Parousia

More Epiphanies from the Mystery of Presence

PHILIP KRILL

authorHOUSE®

AuthorHouse™
1663 Liberty Drive
Bloomington, IN 47403
www.authorhouse.com
Phone: 833-262-8899

Published by AuthorHouse 01/03/2023

ISBN: 978-1-6655-7949-0 (sc)
ISBN: 978-1-6655-7950-6 (e)

Library of Congress Control Number: 2022924104

Print information available on the last page.

To

Nicholas Ayo, C.S.C.

Introduction

This book is a follow-on addition to my previous work, *12 Wicker Baskets: Meditations on the Mystery of Presence*. Presence, it seems, compels us to give expression, in an epiphanic manner, to what is given in the experience of being present.

Presence, I believe, is a simple, immediately accessible entrée into what metaphysicians and theologians call the Mystery of *God*. Presence is not identical with God - what is? Yet Presence is that sophianic handmaid of God - *Hagia Sophia* (Holy Wisdom) - who was *"created at the beginning of God's work"* and who rejoices in God's created world and delights in the human race (Prv. 8:22-31). Presence is the *Sapientia* of God, providing us with a taste of divine bliss otherwise inaccessible to the human heart (cf. 1 Cor. 2:9).

PAROUSIA (π α ρ ο υ σ ί α, parousia) is a Greek term meaning "presence" or "arrival." Because it is used as a technical term in Scripture to refer to the return of Christ in glory at the end of the world, its more immediate, existential impact is often lost. *Presence*, to my mind, restores the epiphanic power of *Parousia*, opening us to the Eternal Now of a divine Fullness (*Plērōma*) that is not yet completely revealed.

I offer this book as an invitation for you to enter more deeply into the mystery of Presence where you may experience the *Parousia* of God. I dedicate this book to my mentor and friend, Nicholas Ayo, C.S.C. who, for nearly 50 years, has shown me what it means to be a person of Presence.

Christmas, 2022

Presence dissolves our problems. At the same time, Presence affords us the wisdom to know intuitively how to manage things that used to baffle us.

Religion is the preferred spiritual fare for those unfamiliar with Presence. Those who practice Presence may still practice religion, but they do so as an extension, not an evasion, of the power of Presence.

The power and permanence of Presence is the taproot of religion. Religion itself is a culturally-driven epiphany that derives from the ineffable Mystery of Presence.

When being present becomes our default mode, we experience the bliss of deification (*theosis*). 'Saints' are those who have made the practice of Presence their permanent *modus operandi*.

Presence is a mystery of letting-go-ness (*Gelassenheit*). In Presence, self-emptying brings self-fulfillment and surrender feels like triumph. In Presence, *kenosis* (self-divestment) is experienced as *theosis* (divinization).

Presence is of a different order from the dualities and polarities of the world. Presence offers the world an alternative to its insanity.

Presence brings divine peace to those who practice it. In Presence, we experience an epiphany of God's peace.

Presence brings peace, joy, and bliss. *Sat* (Being), *Chit* (Awareness), *Bliss* (Ananda) - *Sacchidānanda*.[1]

Worry consumes those who don't know what it means to practice Presence. The choice is simple: the heaven of being present, or the hell of not.

Presence is the epiphany of divine love in a finite world. Presence is the purest form of love we can know.

One person practicing Presence releases more of God's peace into the world than all the actions of the world's do-gooders.

One moment of Presence brings more joy than a lifetime of pleasure.

Presence possesses those who practice it faithfully. In Presence, everything reveals itself as beautiful. Even death appears as a manifestation of an infinite life and love.

---

[1] *Sacchidānanda is* a Hindu term that connotes the divine Bliss (*Ananda*) that arises within us when our Awareness (*Chit*) rests in Being (*Sat*), not in thinking.

In Presence, there are no problems, just as in God 'there is no darkness' (1 Jn. 1:5). Presence banishes our problems, just as light banishes the darkness. All that bedevils us disappears when Presence arises.

Like Dracula fleeing the rising sun, that which troubles us flees before the arising of Presence.

Presence reveals the ego as illusory. Trying to rid oneself of ego is itself an egoic exercise of possessiveness. Presence is possessed of no possessiveness. Possessiveness disappears whenever a person becomes completely present.

Presence presents as a noun but is neither subject nor object. Presence is a Mystery that makes our awareness of subjects and objects possible.

Presence is known in an awareness that is aware of itself. Presence is a transcendental Mystery known in the experience of consciousness conscious of itself. As such, Presence is experienced as elusive, ungraspable, yet as more truly real than both the subjects and objects it includes.

Like bubbles arising in a gently boiling pot, divine intuitions arise spontaneously within Presence, bursting with wisdom and light often too beautiful to express.

True freedom is experienced only in Presence. In Presence, we are free from thoughts and our intuition is unclouded. Wisdom replaces thinking as the source of our inspiration. Without reflection, we intuitively know what to do, or not to do, in the grace of the present moment.

Presence is the amniotic fluid in which creative action is born. Genius inventions come, not when great inventors are thinking of what to do, but through their openness to that which cannot be thought.

When we are present to another, a space opens up that envelops both of us in an embrace of unconditional love and acceptance. Past mistakes and future misgivings evaporate when Presence arises.

Presence makes any task enjoyable. Bliss is no further away than our willingness to give what's immediately at hand our full attention.

We are illumined within by the light of Presence. Looking into the eyes of a person fully present is to glimpse the face of God.

Presence is empty of anything but openness to the Infinite. Presence is devoid of mental or emotional movements towards judgment, analysis or division. Presence is the fullness of Peace and the absence of perturbation.

In Presence, there is neither fear nor evil. In Presence, the beauty of the Infinite is self-evident, causing immediate bliss. Presence is a taste of the perfect love that 'casts out fear' (cf. 1 Jn. 4:18) and 'expels demons' (cf. Mk. 1:34).

Presence is the space in which the actuality of existence is mystically apprehended. In Presence, we have an intuition of uncanniness of being, a felt-sense of the utter fortuity of all that is. It is really quite arresting.

Presence is the place of perpetual childhood. Presence is the virginal point of the Now in which time and space disappear.[2] Presence allows us to traverse the indefinable boundary between time and eternity.

Once in Presence, we never want to leave. Except, in Presence, the notion of 'never' has no meaning. In Presence, there is always only Now. In Presence, we are born anew in every present moment.

Practicing Presence is indulging in awe before the mystery of being. Presence reveals us as *homo adorans* - those who stand in adoring awareness of an ineffable Source greater than ourselves. Presence is the intuitive realization that in God 'we live and move and have our being' (Acts 17:28).

---

[2] See my book, *Le Point Vierge: Meditations on the Mystery of Presence.*

From the vantage point of Presence, we realize, without regret and with no little humor, that our bodies are ultimately given as food for worms. Our garments of flesh are on loan to us to awaken us to our identities in Presence and to show us the transcendental nature of our existence. Some awaken to this awareness only as their bodies are dissolving, some thereafter. Everyone awakens eventually.

Presence is the redemption of guilt, shame and regret. It is the graveyard of our fears, doubts and insecurities. Presence reveals history as held and made perfect in all its twists and turns by a Love so plērōmic as to make what we call 'evil' irrelevant.

It sounds insensitive to say that Presence reveals evil to be nothing more than an illusion of the egoic mind. But so it is. When we dwell intentionally in Presence, we awaken to the realization that, in God, 'all is well and all manner of things shall be well.'[3]

Presence reveals the world perfect in every way, perfect at every moment. All comes from Presence, all returns to Presence, perfectly achieving the purpose for which it is, i.e., for the manifestation and glorification of its self-exteriorizing Source.

One moment of living in Presence releases more healing goodness into the cosmos than a lifetime of social engineering. Nothing done apart from Presence bears fruit that will last.

---

[3] Julian of Norwich, *Revelations of Divine Love.*

Babbling about Presence, apart from saying nothing at all, is the only way to give it adequate expression. The mind short-circuits trying to figure it all out. Presence is the pre-condition for whatever is said or done; thus, nothing that can be said or done can do Presence justice.

Presence is often pictured as an aura, a halo or a penumbra. These are signifiers of its inherent ungraspableness. In Presence, we bask in its light and 'in its light we see light' (cf. Ps. 36:9). But Presence itself is nowhere to be seen.

In Presence, we are happy to leave things unfinished. Presence fills us with a sense that 'less is more.' Nothing seems incomplete. All appears perfect in light of a horizon that makes all things new.

Presence, which possesses us, is as unaffected by our thoughts as the sky is by the passing clouds. Those who ascend beyond their thoughts enter the heaven of Presence.

Presence reveals belief in evil as the root of evil. 'Nothing that is real can be threatened, and nothing unreal exists.'[4] Because it is a privation, evil enjoys no substance, no reality. Ultimately, evil is an illusion - that is, a product of the mind. The problem is, the whole world is hypnotized by it.

---

[4] *Course in Miracles.*

The deeper we enter into Presence, the sillier our questions become. The moment we rise above our thoughts they show themselves as relatively unimportant.

Presence relativizes our thinking instead of wrestling with it. Presence conquers our fears, doubts and insecurities by subversion, not through head-on assault.

Presence is not in competition with our thinking. Presence is the power that allows our thinking to peter itself out. Presence is the compassionate matron who allows the kicking and crying children to fall asleep in her embrace.

Presence is the graveyard where drama and histrionics go to die. Presence is the infinite stillness in which the cries of the anxious receive no response.

Presence is the oven in which the yeast of transcendence turns the dough of our lives into the bread of life. This bread is given 'for the life of the world' (cf. Jn. 6:51).

Everything arises afresh in the mystery of Presence. Presence is the pristine garden in which seeds of contemplation sprout continuously as flowers of beauty, goodness and bliss. The sweet scent of Presence exudes from those who practice it faithfully.

Presence is the sound of silence. All comes from silence, all returns to silence. Presence is wordless, thoughtless consciousness, perfectly alert yet devoid of analysis; exquisitely poised but unperturbed; completely attentive but without agenda. Presence is unrestricted openness to the totality of being, without itself being a part of being.

If the word 'Presence' were used instead of the word 'God,' it would be easier for us to glimpse the Mystery towards which the word 'God' points.

Presence produces fruit within us without any help from us. The fruits of Presence can only be received, not produced. The instant we shift our attention from thinking to being present, Presence transforms us into instruments of peace, simplicity and beauty.

Presence is the nowhere place out of which genius appears. Thinking often acts as a barrier to creativity. Inspiration reveals Presence as the precondition for breakthrough change.

In Presence, we discover that our *desire* to love is purer and more transformative than our *acts* of love. In Presence, we learn what it means to say, 'I cannot not love.' At the same time, we take no credit for the love Presence engenders within us.

Presence tempers our infinite desire for love. Presence turns possessiveness and craving into benignity and genuine affection. Presence introduces a holy relinquishment into our unrestricted desire to love and to be loved.

Sitting with a friend in Presence bonds us more completely than any tangible expressions of affection. Only in Presence can gestures of love become divine. Outside of Presence they become demonic.

In Presence, there is an absence of expectation, anticipation, trepidation and calculation. Presence is the realm of freedom where neither deliberation nor decision is called for. Presence is the space where an intuitive, inexpressible grasp of the truth is given.

Presence envelops us in our woundedness like a good mother whispering gentle assurances to her injured child. Presence quiets the whimpering of our minds and gives our hearts permission to show themselves without fear.

Presence dismantles our character armor and disarms us of our protective shields. Presence ushers us into a space where light dispels darkness, and trust replaces fear.

Presence subverts our resistance and brings to an abrupt halt our objections to anyone or anything. Infinite understanding and infinite forgiveness are the immediate by-products of Presence.

When we are present to anyone or anything, a space is created where communion is possible. Dire situations become less dire. Tragic situations become less tragic. Hope and joy arise naturally in Presence. The advent of Presence promises redemption to even the most unfortunate circumstances.

Presence is the space of personal integration. Presence strips us of our egoic identity and leads us into *who* we are apart from *what* we are. Our true identities are 'hidden in God' (cf. Col. 3:3) but intuited in Presence.

In Presence, neither doubts nor fears nor questions arise. The epiphany of being that arises in Presence quells all such doubts and fears and questions. Presence shows us that the answer to all questions is, ultimately, there are no questions.

Time and space exist only outside of Presence. The challenge is to move about in time and space enveloped in Presence. Even the angels move out of the way when they see a person walking in Presence.

Persons living in Presence project a benign indifference to the problems of the world, yet exhibit deep compassion for those who are hurting. They recognize that pain is real but evil an illusion. Because they are in possession of a peace 'the world cannot give' (cf. Jn. 14:27) they know the futility of trying to make the world a better place. They know that Presence is the only place we can truly live. They have learned how to live 'in the world but not be of the world' (cf. Jn. 15:19).

Presence is 'the pearl of great price' (Mt. 13:46). Those who have found it forsake all else to possess it. Yet Presence cannot be possessed; it possesses us. We awaken to Presence as the Source of our own capacity to be present.

Our effusiveness about Presence, exhausting itself with words like these, brings us back to Presence. Singing the praises of Presence, we return to Presence, frustrated in our efforts to give it expression. Coming or going, we always return to the place of unspeakable Presence.

In Presence, we acquire the innocent attentiveness of a little child. Our attention is continually arrested by the here and now. Past and future vanish, problems disappear. We realize the present moment is all there is. There is nothing more to desire.

Presence is the space in which our problems lose their steam. In Presence, we calm down enough to see clearly. Peace and wisdom arise naturally when we become present.

Presence is the fulcrum with which Archimedes claimed he could lift the world. He never realized, perhaps, that this fulcrum works from within, not from without.

Presence is a letting go that is simultaneously a filling up. Presence empties us of thinking and fills us with mindfulness.

In the light of mindfulness, we can see our thoughts and actions more clearly. In Presence, we perceive ourselves from a standpoint beyond ourselves. Yet this standpoint beyond ourselves is also our deepest self.

Presence, uncreated and without beginning or end, is the primordial Source of all that is, and Presence is that *in which* all that is abides.

Everything that is is capable of experiencing and manifesting Presence in accord with its own nature. Each object also enjoys its own measure of self-presence. It's possible, says Annie Dillard, to teach even a stone to talk.[5]

The Mystery of Presence shows itself most visibly in our capacity for *self-presence*. Our experience of self-transcendence reveals both our identity with and difference from the power of Presence which possesses us.

Our experience of ourselves as persons is the manifestation of Presence within us. Presence is the fontal Source of all that is personal. Presence makes our encounters even with so-called inanimate matter quasi-personal. This is why St. Francis could speak with such love to 'sister moon and brother sun.'

---

[5] Annie Dillard, *Teaching a Stone to Talk*. Cf. Lk. 19:40.

Presence is the redemption of every object placed within it. Thoughts and feelings are redeemed in Presence just as much as a tragic car accident. Placed in Presence, the pain and suffering of life's countless disappointments are drawn out as if from a sore body placed in a hot bath of Epsom salts.

Presence reveals being and knowing as coincident in a single Source greater than both.

It is impossible to get behind or ahead of Presence. It is always there, both before and after we arrive.

Presence is like an interior shadow which, instead of following us around like our external shadow, leads us ever more deeply into the present moment. Presence is the light that leads us ever forward, dispelling any darkness that seems to threaten us.

Presence reveals being as a mystery intensely alive and personal. Presence shows us the fortuity of our existence, the unspeakable uncanniness of all that is. Presence disarms us with an intuition of the gratuity of being.

Silence is the language of Presence. Stillness pervades and encompasses all that is. Recognizing the core of our existence as Presence, we bask in its silence. Yet this silence is intensely alive because the Presence from which it comes and to which it returns is the Source of life itself.

All that exists participates in Presence as its transcendent Source. Existence vibrates at its core with an ineffable energy not of its own making. Presence is the power flowing from a Source beyond words and human comprehension. Some call this Source 'God.' The closest we can come to God in this world is to experience Presence.

In Presence, we are reduced to silence. Silence is at once the condition for and result of Presence.

Presence is the destruction of egoic existence. Ego is the cocoon of unconsciousness that keeps human beings somnambulant. Presence transforms human caterpillars into human butterflies.

Presence is a transcendental experience of sharing in a Power greater than ourselves with which we are simultaneously one and distinct. In Presence, we transcend ourselves without leaving or losing ourselves. Presence is at once our own deepest personal identity and a Power that precedes and exceeds it.

Presence envelops our experience and drains it of drama. Presence neutralizes our anxiety and bathes everything in an indefinable but benevolent light. Presence takes the edge off of evil, while allowing us to see it for what it is, i.e. an illusion of the egoic mind.

Presence imparts clarity of vision, banishing the clouded judgments that wreck havoc upon our emotions. Presence frees us from our fears and imparts wisdom. In Presence, we learn how to negotiate life in a non-reactive way.

Presence is a world beyond good and evil. Presence is a power that transcends morality while also imparting a connaturality for doing what's good and beautiful and right. Presence is what ethical behavior aims at achieving but can never attain.

Presence arrests. It stops fear, doubt and insecurity in their steps. The inner stillness of a person practicing Presence calms a crisis with a simple look, and defuses anger with a mere softening of the eyes. Presence brings peace wherever it arises.

Presence and self-possession go hand-in-hand. In Presence, the true self is not lost, but is found, in Presence. Presence strips us of the cosmetics of ego, revealing our hidden, beautiful, true selves under the phony make-up.

Presence is the true fountain of youth. Those who practice Presence grow younger, never older. They recover the childlike innocence, together with a supernatural wisdom, that makes them fit for the kingdom. of God (cf. Lk. 18:17).

Presence is a bottomless wellspring of inspiration. Those who think or write, speak or act from Presence do so with a voice and a style more graceful than their own. Presence takes possession of such persons and uses them as instruments of its redemptive design.

Those who practice Presence embody the desire of the poet: 'I am a hole in a flute through which the Christ's breath moves - listen to this music.'[6]

Poise follows from Presence. A person or an animal who is poised maintains an alert, hyper-aware, discerning openness to the mystery of the present moment. Nothing can flummox one poised in Presence.

If Presence is the deepest Source of our existence, then divine bliss is our natural state of being. Ego beclouds this bliss but this bliss is restored the moment we shift from thinking to Presence. It's impossible to be in Presence and not be infused with bliss.

The bliss of Presence is the result of intuiting being as an altogether unnecessary gift. The Giver of this gift is indirectly apprehended in Presence.

Presence takes us beyond the dualities that bedevil our understanding: good vs. evil, reason vs. faith, natural vs. supernatural, right vs. wrong.

---

[6] Hafiz, *The Gift*.

Presence prohibits debate. Presence disarms us of our propensity for polarization. In Presence, we discover that being unable to argue is better than winning the argument. The games of tit-for-tat are finished when, in Presence, we stop playing. The peace of Presence is automatic and disarming.

Those who enter Presence do so as those entering a cool cathedral. The enormity, beauty and sacred stillness there makes us forget the heated, petty world left at the door. Settling into the refreshing stillness of the cathedral of Presence, we never want to leave.

Moving from thinking to Presence is the simplest, yet most subtle and difficult shift a person can make. Everyone does it unintentionally each time the thought process is arrested or momentarily interrupted. When any event interrupts our mental cogitations, we are catapulted briefly into that blessed space of spontaneous, unthinking awareness. Usually these moments of arrested attention pass very quickly and the effort of analysis resumes its relentless grind.

Presence reveals the world of functional impetuousness - of plans and schedules and deadlines and built-in expectations - as a house of cards and a pack of lies. There are nothing but artifacts in the world of functionality, but in Presence everything is natural, organic, beautifully spontaneous. In Presence, the world becomes a kaleidoscope, revealing an ever-changing, ever-more-beautiful horizon 'in which we live and move and have our being' (Acts 17:28).

Presence saves us from being submerged in the demands and routines of the workaday world. Presence is the cool breeze taking the edge of our heated moments. Presence is the permanent, ever-present oasis to which we can retreat when trudging doggedly through the desert of life.

Presence reveals death to be, neither the opposite nor the equal of life, but its siamese twin. Presence is simultaneously death and resurrection. In Presence, we die to control and arise in freedom. In Presence, we die to presumption and power and rise in unexpected bliss. Presence is our liberation from the 'slavery to the fear of death' (cf. Heb. 2:15).

Presence is the manifestation of the cosmos' final *Plērōma* within the conditions of time and space. Presence is the appearance of the Whole within each of the universe's parts.

Presence is the experience of the end in the beginning and the beginning in the end. It's as if the acorn and the oak have revealed themselves in stereoscopic harmony. Presence is an anticipatory fullness (*plērōma*), a satisfied yearning.

In Presence, we discern the perfection of the whole amidst the assembling and dissolution of the parts. In Presence, we intuit an ultimate joy within the agonistic movements of concrete existence. In Presence, we apprehend the priority of resurrected splendor within death and destruction.

Presence alights from the still point within our spirit, that indefinable infinite abyss, that is at once the epicenter and circumference of our existence. Presence reveals us as unique, irreplaceable, unsubstitutable images and likenesses of itself. Presence imbues us with an identity that is both derived and distinct from itself.

Presence can be experienced but never thought. Presence is real but never objective. Presence has no body but informs all bodies. Presence is never seen but makes understanding possible. Presence never changes but allows us to appreciate change.

Presence melts our defenses. Presence softens our eyes and hearts. Presence relaxes our grip on life.

Presence is the space in which we let go and discover the truth about ourselves. Presence is the space of *Gelassenheit* (relinquishment) in which all things appear as they are, not as our ego would have them.

Presence reveals the transcendental nature of personal identity. In Presence, we learn to disidentify with any definitions of ourselves. We take a step back from ourselves and catch a glimpse of our true selves. Yet, our true self eludes objectification. It is an identity hidden in the Mystery of Presence.

In Presence, is impossible for us to politicize. Presence reveals every form of national, racial, ideological, sexual (or trans-sexual) identification as an exercise in egoic illusion. Politics is the world's mimetic violence in which the insane logic of group identification crucifies Presence.

Our capacity to dis-identify with any descriptions or objectifications of ourselves is our inherent nature as persons acting in a perfectly divine manner. What believers call 'God' is a primordial Mystery of self-dis-identifcation, an aboriginal Mystery of self-transcendence, an ineffable Source of ungraspable Presence.

What Christians call 'Trinity' is the God who transcends Himself within Himself. The Father (Source) transcends Himself eternally in the begetting of the Son (Word). The Son 'does not deem equality with God (Source) as something to be grasped at but empties himself' in an act of self-transcendence mirroring that of the Father (cf. Phil. 2:6-11). The mutual self-surrender of Father (Source) and Son (Word) issues forth in a *Penumbra* of Presence (Spirit), enfolding and perfecting this primordial Mystery of self-transcendence. Our experience of Presence is a participation in the self-transcending - and therefore self-dis-identification - of Father, Son, and Holy Spirit.

Presence delivers us from the wasteland of morality and ethics. Ethics is what happens when Presence is lost. In Presence, one needs no guidance about the right thing to do or say. In Presence, wisdom replaces deliberation, intuition supersedes calculation.

In Presence, we experience a rebirth of childlike innocence infused with an arresting depth of discernment. We become 'as wise as serpents and as innocent as doves' (cf. Mt. 10:16). Presence imbues us with eternal youth and ancient wisdom.

Presence acts as an internal governor upon our impulses and actions. It shows us when to move and when to do nothing. It neutralizes the chatter in our heads and unveils the wisdom of the heart. It cautions us not to move until we see it, and it compels us to act once we do. Presence is our infallible guide on our journey through life.

Presence brings forth infinite compassion. Viewed in the light of Presence, every person appears beautiful. Presence turns criticism into kindness, judgment into understanding. At the same time, our awareness of evil - i.e., the lack of Presence in ourselves and others - is made more acute. We become both more benevolent and more discerning, more caring and more careful. In Presence, our compassion acquires a dimension of prudence that keeps gentleness from becoming gullibility and getting us in trouble.

Presence is at once intimate and infinite, immediate yet without beginning or end. In Presence, we experience the unconditioned act of our existence as emanating from a Source that is both immanent and transcendent.

Presence is the immediate Source of all being but is not another being among beings. Presence is the power of the Now/Tao that always was, is, and always will be.

Presence is the space of forgiveness. Presence envelops and transcends 'the good and bad alike, both the just and the unjust' (cf. Mt. 5:45). Once awakened in Presence, no kettle will ever call any pot black. In the crystal palace of Presence, no one throws stones.

Presence arises from an indefinable, Archimedean point within our being. The opening of this virginal point within us fills both our body and soul with a Light and Presence from beyond ourselves. It is our point of connection between our life and the life of God.

Presence is electric with the power of actuality. Presence is an existential apprehension of the Infinite - as something at once immediate and transcendent. The reality of Presence is lost on those who have not made the shift from thinking to simple, limpid, spacious awareness.

Presence is devoid of ideas but filled with attentiveness. Presence is poise on steroids.

Presence is an awareness of our absolute dependence upon a Source greater than, distinct from, yet one with ourselves. Presence is an existential intuition of an unnameable, transcendent, unconditioned Origin of being. This Source constitutes the being of every created being, yet is 'other' from all that is made.

Jesus says, 'I AM the Way, the Truth and the Life' (Jn. 14:6). But what if he meant: 'I AM *is* the Way, the Truth and the Life? If this is the case, then our 'I-am-ness' is a divinizing participation in the One who calls himself 'I AM.' We are they who are *in* Him who is I AM.

It is the 'is-ing-ness' of things that awakens us to the mystery of Presence. Presence is the answer to the perennial philosophical question, 'Why is there something rather than nothing?'

Presence reveals that there is no such thing as nothing. 'Nothing' does not exist. Every so-called 'absence' is but another form of Presence. Evil is an illusion of the mind quickly dispelled once the difference between thinking and Presence is discovered.

Presence gives us a deifying taste of eternal life. Presence is the elixir for all that ails us. It is the fountain of eternal youth sought by all generations.

Presence is alert stillness. It is perfect poise. Presence is acutely focused yet completely relaxed. The eyes of a person practicing Presence are as soft as they are keen.

Presence is bereft of judgment and condemnation. In Presence, there is no accusation, judgment or condemnation. It is impossible for anyone steeped in Presence to judge, condemn or accuse another. It's not that they decide not to do it, but that the divinizing power of Presence makes such an action impossible. It's only when a person returns to thinking that judging begins anew.

There is no difference between abiding in Presence for a lifetime or entering it for the first time. The experience of Presence is always an experience absolutely new, absolutely fresh.

Presence is the eternal Now breaking into time and space rendering both past and future irrelevant to the bliss of the present moment. In Presence, all things are made new (Rev. 21:5).

Advice-giving has no place in Presence. In Presence, everyone minds his or her own business. At the same time, in Presence we empathize with the sufferings of others as never before.

Presence is the redemption of loneliness. Presence converts loneliness into solitude. Solitude is solicitous of everyone but solicits no one.

Presence makes us comfortable with ourselves so we can live comfortably with others. In Presence, we are never less alone than when we are with ourselves.

Being steeped in Presence is the opposite of being submerged in a crowd. Succumbing to peer pressure is death to those seeking to live in Presence. Practicing Presence immunizes us against spiritual death.

Presence is a space of both emptiness and fulfillment. Letting go and being suffused with joy, peace, and compassion are a single mystery - the mystery of being present.

The experience of Presence is an abyss of ever-greater, ever-deeper levels of letting go and being filled. In Presence, death and life are synonymous. Presence is the Paschal Mystery compacted into a single, indefinable nowhere point from which all being, consciousness and bliss are begotten.

Presence is appreciating the here and now as revealing the face of God. In Presence, our breath is taken away by the beauty and utterly fortuitous giftedness of the present moment. Pure, attentive, accepting awareness of being is bliss: *Sacchidānanda.*[7]

Discontent dissolves in the space of Presence. Nothing but love abides in Presence. Presence is impervious to evil and reveals ethics as a silly game practiced only by those who know nothing of Presence.

---

[7] See above, n. 1.

Presence is an experience of continual rebirth - a perpetual movement 'from one degree of glory to another' (cf. 2. Cor. 3:18). When we've abided Presence ten thousand years, it will be as if we have just begun.[8]

Presence is an ever-expanding experience of redemption. Every instant of Presence is a deeper purification and perfection of the previous one. In Presence, God appears as 'all in all' (cf. Eph. 1:23; 4:6).

Presence allows us to both acknowledge and accept unhappiness. Presence envelops unhappiness in its arms and allows it to cry itself to sleep.

Presence is the answer to human violence. Imagine a mad man punching the air. Presence is the life-giving air, the man, humanity punching itself out. Presence proves itself more powerful than all the violence in the world.

Presence works like epsom salts: it draws the soreness out of being hurtfully human. Presence keeps otherness from becoming alienation; difference from being destructive; alterity from becoming isolation or alienation. Presence is the great healer. It provides salve for the wounds inflicted by the slings and arrows of our outrages fortunes.

Presence is a dynamic space of perpetually transcending immanence. In Presence, the immediate is affirmed as partaking of the infinite.

---

[8] Words of the hymn, *Amazing Grace*.

The experience of Presence is continual bliss. Stepping outside of Presence into unconscious anxiety is the definition of hell.

Hell, and the suffering it entails, is subversive of itself. Suffering, taken to the extreme, eventually occasions an internal letting-go that is an opening to the peace of Presence. It's impossible to travel to the depths of hell without discovering the entrance to heaven.

Presence is disarming in its simplicity. It is sharing in the simplicity and compassionate aseity of God.

Presence is a fullness of actuality that can be neither threatened or destroyed. Presence is the invisible port available in every storm, the elusive refuge in every crisis.

Presence is the pause in the harangue, the gap between our thoughts. Presence is discovered in the stillness that settles in after the chaos has calmed.

Presence conveys the love of God, even to those who don't believe in God. Neither a rant against God nor the praise of God speaks as truly about God as does simply being present.

God is as undeniable as mystery of Presence, for in denying it one presumes it. Yet there are many who have not yet discovered how to be knowingly present, who have not yet discovered the power of Presence. The hell of atheism exists only until the the heavenly bliss of Presence is experienced.

A certain *fiat* (assent) is required for Presence to give itself. Everyone experiences Presence unintentionally throughout the day whenever thinking stops and a break in the action occurs. Yet to intentionally 'be present,' we must consciously 'step back' from the continuous flow of thoughts and emotions that flood our minds and hearts. An intentional 'letting go, 'stepping away,' 'taking a deep breath,' or 'taking a time out' must take place in which we 'get ahold of ourselves' and 'take a look at ourselves.' Presence arises when we become our own self-observers. Suddenly, we become aware that our consciousness is self-transcendent and that this power of self-transcendence derives from a power of Presence greater than ourselves.

We never possess Presence. Presence always arises as a gift. Our desire to 'be present' is the power of Presence awakening us to a gift that is forever ours. Presence possesses us, never us it.

Presence reveals itself as the benevolent overseer of our thinking process. Presence, as it were, smiles at us when we become lost in our thoughts. When we awaken to the egoic silliness of our mental machinations, we experience Presence. This awakening always has something light-hearted about it, like an all-loving grandparent smiling, with soft eyes, at a grandchild frustrated with its efforts to achieve.

Presence is the source of true relaxation. Being present is a letting go that goes all the way down. When we void ourselves of ideas and expectations, our emptiness becomes a fullness of love, into which any evil could be placed and easily redeemed.

Presence is the womb of wisdom. In Presence, we swim in the amniotic fluid of Holy *Sophia*. In Presence, we are reborn and become children fit for the 'kingdom of God' (cf. Mt. 18:3).

Presence is a prophetic space. Abiding in Presence, truth comes from us with a clarity and a convincingness otherwise impossible. In Presence, we speak and act with authority, not as those who speak and act in ego (cf. Mt. 7:29).

Presence is either the great uniter or the great divider. Relationships are either divinized or destroyed when one of the parties begins to live mindfully in Presence. Presence in one person either awakens Presence in the other or compels the other to double down on egoic resistance. One who has tasted Presence can never go back to the way things used to be.

Presence reveals gentleness as the heart of who we are. Immersed in Presence, we become 'as wise as serpents and gentle as lambs' (cf. Mt. 10:16).

The desert has a visceral attraction for a person practicing Presence. Presence kindles a burning desire to be alone with the Alone. At the same time, Presence opens us in compassion to all those dying of thirst in the workaday world.

Presence gives us patience impossible to achieve by our own effort. All virtues, including patience, arise in Presence as by-products of being present. Ethics are shown to be a Sisyphean illusion in light of the divinizing power of Presence.

Presence is a space of blessed impoverishment. Bereft of thoughts or agenda, we are made wealthy with an openness and compassion surpassing every created good. Poverty and *Plērōma* (divine fullness) are identical in Presence.

Presence is a participation in the nothingness of God. God is no-thing, a non-subsistent Mystery of self-diffusive actuality. Presence is the sophianic self-communication of God, making us instrumental icons of His own divine actuality.

Presence renders us indifferent to the opinions of others. In Presence, criticism has no power to tear us down, nor praise to build us up. The prophetic power of Presence is such that it inures us to outside commentary, while making us alive to the needs of others.

Presence is a proleptic participation in the final *telos* (purpose) and *plērōma* (fullness) of of creation. Presence is a theophanic vision which, far from generating grandiosity, engenders within us the deepest humility and gratitude. In this space of ecstatic expectation which is Presence, even the most seemingly insignificant things in life are experienced as bathed in the light of eternity.

Like an electrical transformer converts overwhelming wattage into a register compatible with our appliances, Presence modulates the unutterable Source of divine Actuality (God) into a frequency that allows us to attune ourselves to it. Presence is the governor on God's infinite creative energy that enables us to enter it, not for our destruction, but for our deification.

Presence is the sophianic medium that makes possible the blissful self-communication of God. Presence is a mystical ethos in which we experience the power of God without dissolution or destruction (cf. Ex. 33:20). Presence is the filter through which God gives us a share in His divinity, and the magnet through which we give God the whole of our humanity.

Presence is the pneumatic tube through which God powerfully draws us up to Himself, only to return us to this world as instruments of His deifying peace.

The longer we abide in Presence the happier we become. Presence rejoices everything it touches. It's as if 'the stones themselves cry for joy' when we walk the road in Presence (cf. Lk. 19:40).[9]

Presence is the bottomless, undisturbed pond which engulfs and quiets everything dropped into it. Presence is as unlimited and unassuming as it is calm and deep. In Presence, being and knowing are the same. In Presence, we 'know as we are known' (cf. 1 Cor. 13:12). In Presence, our awareness of the gift of being is bliss (*Sacchidānanda*).

Presence is to thinking what a room is to the furniture placed within it. The space of Presence is unaffected by the objects that occupy it. Presence is as indifferent to the moral or intellectual status of those who enter into it as air is to those who inhabit it.

It's the power of Presence in a guru, teacher or preacher that touches the hearts of the listeners, not the content of their words. Words, to be meaningful, function as sacraments of Presence, not simply as instruments of communication.

Presence is infinitely unassuming. It begins with the smallest act of letting go and deepens into an ocean of buoyant surrender. In Presence, we discover that letting go means being lifted up, that surrender allows our eternal self to rise to the surface.

---

[9] See above, n. 3.

Presence is the opposite of, and our antidote to, possessiveness. Covetousness - the root of all evil - evaporates in Presence. It is impossible to abide in Presence and continue to crave anything or anyone.

Presence is the miracle of simultaneous self-dispassion and self-actualization. In Presence, the egoic self disappears and the eternal child within shows her face. Soft eyes is a sure sign that a person is abiding in Presence.

Presence is as elusive and immediate as God Himself. Presence is to thinking as God is to the world.

There is no connection between cognition and Presence. Presence (or pure consciousness) is the condition for the possibility of cognition, not its product. We can't think our way into Presence. Once the shift from thinking to Presence is made, however, our thinking becomes more than thinking - it becomes wisdom.

Presence is experienced anew every time it is entered into. In Presence, we become as little children. Presence is a space of awe and wonder, not of thought and reflection. In Presence, we are born again, and again, as children of the light.

Presence is the greatest gift we can give another. Presence is what makes our beneficent actions sacramental, not just exercises in sentimentality. Compared with the gift of Presence, politeness is platitudinous.

Presence disarms demons. That is, demonization cannot withstand the power of Presence. It is impossible to be present and speak ill of another. The demons of gossip, criticism, blame and shame are driven out by Presence.

Presence is a space of perfect peace. Presence accepts everything while rejecting nothing. Presence reveals evil as the impulse to define something or someone else as evil. Thinking indicts, Presence redeems.

Presence transmutes anger into grief, irritation into empathy. Presence allow us to view character faults more with compassion than consternation. Presence takes the edge off of our impatience. Presence tones down our perfectionism. Presence is God's dramamine for our seasick psyches.

Presence shows us that God's timing is always perfect. Nothing is given in Presence that is not given in the present moment, just as we need it, just when we need it.

Every foreground has a background. Every object is situated within a wider horizon. Presence is the unthematic Background of all possible backgrounds, the transcendent Horizon of all conceivable horizons.

In Presence, that which is known is always shown, not told. Wisdom arises unexpectedly as a gift in Presence. It shimmers with a certain charisma absent in simple cognition.

Presence is the cure for intellectual pride. That which is shown in Presence appears more worthy of praise than of possession. Presence reveals human nature to be that of *homo adorans,* not *homo sapien* or *homo faber.*

In Presence, everything is epiphanic. Awakening to wisdom in Presence is being illumined by a series of anagogical eruptions.

To write or speak about Presence is worse than useless unless each and every word flows directly from Presence. Writing a book about Presence is an exercise in learned humility, not anything to be proud of or take credit for.

In Presence, we develop a kind of spiritual Alzheimer's: memories of our past accomplishments and misdeeds fade into nothingness. Instead, our spirits are infused with a kind of ancient-yet-ever-new wisdom that makes us 'as innocent as children and as worldly-wise as serpents' (cf. Mt. 10:16).

Stay in your head too long and you'll find mendacity and malice. Abide in Presence for a single moment and you'll experience only mirth and mercy.

There is no other guru or spiritual guide than Presence. Anyone we call our teacher is taught by being present. All teachers are purveyors, not of information or knowledge, but of wisdom, and only to the degree they are possessed of Presence.

Presence operates in true spiritual guides like music in a virtuoso: it plays them, they don't play it.

True spiritual teachers seek emptiness of mind, much like hermits seek the empty desert. In the emptiness of self-transcending availability, what the teacher is given to say is always and only that - given. Presence is the virginal womb in which divine wisdom is immaculately conceived.

Presence and self-possession are identical, as are Presence and self-dis-possession. Presence is the holographic medium wherein both the dissolution of our ego and the emergence of our true identity occur. Presence imparts both supreme confidence and utter humility. In Presence, we receive ourselves as a gift from a Source greater than ourselves.

The moment we move from thinking to simply noticing, Presence arises.

In Presence, we are like a little child taking a bath. We want it never to end.

The strength imparted by Presence is greater than any worldly power. Presence is the power of a Void, conquering the antagonisms of the world like a pool of water saps the strength of those doing water aerobics, or as the shadow outlasts the shadow boxer. Presence is the power of infinite patience. Presence is the fullness of non-resisting love.

Presence is the experience of self-transcendence intimating a Reality beyond itself. Presence shows us that we carry within us a Power that is at once the Source of our existence and the *Plērōma* of who and what we are.

The fact that we can stand back from ourselves and judge our lives reveals that our deepest identity is participation in a Presence that both precedes and prompts our desire to do so. Presence is a continually arresting, amazing and defining experience for those who know what it is really all about.

Our experience of Presence confirms Teilhard de Chardin's aphorism that 'we are not human beings having a spiritual experience but spiritual beings having a human experience.'

The fact that we can place the whole of our memories and recollections into Presence shows us that we are not only *more* than whatever those memories say about us, but, in a fundamental sense, *unrelated* to those recollections. There is within us, in other words, a hidden identity (cf. Col. 3:3), which is purer and more primordial than memory.

In Presence, we encounter a power of consciousness that is beyond cognition, judgment and representation. Presence is beyond dialectic and sublation, beyond dualities and polarities.

An invitation to practice Presence is like being asked to play music on a soundless piano. Presence is the silent music of heaven.

Presence keeps the mystery of being from devolving into a philosophical problem. Our minds are never troubled when immersed in Presence.

Presence grants us the gift of eternal youth. We grow younger, never older, when abiding in Presence. Presence is the womb of rebirth unto eternal childhood.

In Presence, we realize, with pure joy, that we will always be learners. We bow before Presence as beginners before a Zen master. Our willingness to listen and learn, no matter what the cost, brings us divine bliss. When we've practiced Presence for ten thousand years it will be as if we have just begun.[10]

Presence is a kaleidoscope of beauty, every turn of which brings an upshot of bliss greater than the one before.

---

[10] See above, n. 7.

Presence mutes only the interpretive elements of human thinking; otherwise, Presence expands our register for discernment and sharpens our ability to make wise and prudent decisions.

Presence is beyond dialectics, divisions and debates. It is also beyond polarities, paradoxes and opposites. Presence is a mystery *non aliud*: so completely 'other' as to be 'other than anything other,' or 'not-other.' Presence is not in competition with anything but illumines the beauty of everything.

Abiding in Presence can be compared with nothing else we do, but everything we do is incomparably better when done in Presence.

Presence eliminates our tendency to compare, replacing it with insatiable gratitude. To compare is to despair. To abide in Presence is to delight in the eternal Now.

Presence cannot be reduced to a discreet act of intentional awareness. Sadists and sociopaths exhibit intentional awareness in their acts of malevolence. Presence is an awareness of our own awareness in such a self-transcending way that we are necessarily prevented from doing deliberate or intentional harm. Presence is so teleologically beautiful, and immerses us in such anticipatory bliss, as to make those who experience it incapable of evil.

In Presence, our need for deliberate decision making disappears. The deliberative will is summoned only when our practice of Presence is forfeited to analytical thinking. In Presence, those who know, know they know nothing; yet, they also know they are in possession of a wisdom 'passing all understanding' (cf. Php. 4:7).

We abide in Presence always as its servant, not as its owner. Presence is always experienced as a gift, the gift that never stops giving.

Our voraciousness for Presence is matched only by our gratitude in receiving it. Presence is the end of our greediness and the 'fulfillment of all desire' (cf. Ps. 20:4).

Presence unmasks our pride, self-hatred and despair not as evil but as petty. Presence never indicts what seems amiss but subverts it with humor and humility.

Presence is the ineluctably tacit dimension of our existence and our experience. Before I am this or that, *I am*. Before I know myself as this or that, I am aware that *I am*. Our awareness of our 'I-am-ness,' even when made an object of our focal attention, is present also, and irreducibly, as a background of tacit awareness.

Even when we live knowingly in Presence, the tacit dimension of Presence infinitely exceeds our conscious awareness. In Presence, 'we live and move and have our being' (Acts 17:28). To say we can never separate ourselves from Presence is saying too little.

Practicing Presence affords us but a peek into the unfathomable mystery of Presence. Yet, one such peek makes the rest of our perceptions seem like self-hypnosis.

Presence is not passivity. It is a space of alert attentiveness without agenda. Presence is an experience of transcendental openness to we-know-not-what. Yet, the 'know-not-what' of this orientation is the Source and fulfillment of its teleological aim.

Presence is the opposite of stoic detachment or oriental indifference. Presence is an intentional relaxation into the embrace of the present moment. Entering Presence is a letting go that is simultaneously an opening up. Presence is an deliberate relinquishment of expectations in anticipation of transcendental peace.

Presence is infinitely creative. Devoid of intellection, Presence generates intuitive ingenuity, creative genius. Even the very best craftspersons receive their inspiration from a place deeper and more indefinable than their planning process. That place is Presence.

Everything emerging from Presence has a note of otherness about it. The fruits of Presence are always asymmetrical with what the world considers satisfying. Creative genius flourishes in Presence, but creative geniuses are often scorned when first expressing their breakthrough ideas. They don't care because in Presence they have found 'the one thing needful' (cf. Lk. 10:42).

Presence engenders a fierce yet humble fidelity. Fidelity to Presence can overcome infidelity in relationships, but never vice versa.

Ignorance or forgetfulness of Presence is the root cause of the world's problems.

Principles cannot inspire fidelity like Presence can. Principles appeal to the head, Presence to the heart. Such a distinction seems artificial only to those already too much compromised by intellection.

Those who speak, write about or attempt to preach about Presence always do so as 'unworthy servants' (cf. Lk. 17:10). One cannot abide in Presence and remain the least bit proud.

In Presence, the social order appears as collective hubris, collective insanity.

Presence is neither abstract nor impersonal. Presence is the dissolution of the ego, not the person. Nothing is disowned in Presence. Instead a true identity is revealed, but one which cannot be defined or objectified in any way. One's true colors, as it were, do not fade into nothingness but become unimaginably more radiant in Presence. In Presence, all is purified and enhanced, not blurred into abstraction.

Presence is the opposite of conformism. Presence engenders an active resistance to interior dissipation. Presence will not allow a person to surrender to routine. Presence is God's cure for spiritual sclerosis.

It's in Presence that we catch a glimpse of the faces we had before we were born. Presence reveals our eternal childhood.

Presence unveils a world beyond the problematical. Presence reminds us that prior to understanding there is an astonishment at being. In Presence, we are arrested by the mystery of existence.

Presence beholds the beauty even of that which seems off kilter. Presence bathes all in a penumbra of divine radiance.

In Presence, we acquire the emotional equivalent of a safecracker's touch. In Presence, we learn how to handle things so gently that they open of their own accord.

Practicing Presence issues in an incitement to create. Inspirations appear as if by magic when we give ourselves over to Presence. It's as if the on-going creativity of God possesses those who practice Presence.

Presence engenders a quiet but fierce fidelity in those possessed of it. It exercises a hold on us different from our addictive attachments. Presence exerts an allure, an invitation to a hidden tryst in the eternal Now. It compels us but doesn't coerce us to follow its call.

Presence puts us in a kind of permeable state. We open ourselves, without judgment, to what is, to what arrives as pure gift.

Benevolence is the ethos of Presence. It is a virginal space in which our nuptial communion with reality takes place.

When we meet another in Presence, they become, as it were, a part of us. A kind of 'communion of saints' is constellated in which the other is forever with us, even if the other is absent or dead and gone. Objects are forgettable, but anything or anyone encountered in Presence remains with us always. Presence is the power of eternal with-ness.

Confrontation, argumentation, accusation, sarcasm, cynicism, criticism and even certain forms of questioning are anathema in Presence, but Presence anathematizes nothing. Instead, Presence is the space where egoic outbursts are accepted and dissolved.

Presence is a graveyard of melodrama and histrionics.

Presence is inherently personal and relational. In Presence, we experience a mystery that is self-communicative. It's as if the whole of our being is open and extended outward to a Power that draws us into itself. Presence is always experienced as an encounter with the Infinite.

We feel intimately known in Presence. The experience of Presence is like being drawn into an unnameable embrace of supra-personal love. In Presence, we know that we are known better than we know ourselves (cf. 1 Cor. 13:12). We can't believe the joy.

Presence is a state of total spiritual availability (*disponsibilité*). It is a state of intentional docility, purposeful innocence. In Presence, we acquire a second naiveté that is wise to, but not worried about, the ways of the world. In Presence, we are in the world but not of it (cf. Jn, 15:19).

Presence disposes us naturally to others, and others to us. Presence is self-communicative and attractive. When we are possessed of Presence, others feel naturally inclined to confide in us. We become open invitations for the other's self-disclosure. Presence creates a field of accepting attentiveness that is healing for all who enter it.

Presence is what makes the difference between a saint and a social worker.

Presence is something more elusive and indefinable than conscientious listening. Presence is bereft of effort. 'Duty' has no place in Presence. Presence knows nothing of obligation. Presence communicates gratuity, goodness and grace; freedom, joy and gladness. Presence makes us glad to be with another without a reason. Presence is a why-less love.

Presence is an ethos of holy communion. Presence is automatic self-dispossession in deference to the other. Love flows like electricity as soon as we plug into Presence.

In Presence, we give the other not just our attention but ourselves. Presence is never without an invisible smile, a light in the eyes, levity in the heart. Presence is joyous attentiveness, a gaze always more grateful than grave.

Presence is an indefinable connection, often conveyed simply with a smile, a handshake, an intonation. We know it when we see it, even if its definition eludes us.

Presence is the essence of the I-Thou relationship. In Presence, heart speaks to heart, even where no words are exchanged. *Cor ad cor loquitur.*

Presence is radical reciprocity, but not a 'this-for-that.' Presence is mutual space-making. Attentive, loving silence is at the heart of the self-dispossession that occurs in Presence.

Presence is undivided, unqualified availability to the other. Such availability overcomes alienation. We are alienated from others to the extent that we are not present to them. It's not possible to pretend Presence or to pretend *in* Presence.

We can feign sympathy or empathy, but not Presence. The discerning eye can tell. If we practice Presence, sympathy and empathy that make a difference occur naturally. Presence is the end of pretending.

Presence is without any sense of obligation, save the felt-obligation to abide in Presence as knowingly and continuously as possible. Presence beckons, never commands. There is no 'supposed to' in Presence. We are not really present when we tell ourselves, 'I'm supposed to be present here.' Either we are present or we are not. There is no middle ground.

Presence is purity of heart.

In Presence, we experience things exactly as they are supposed to be. Or, rather, in Presence we cannot imagine things being other than the way they are at the present moment. Judgments about 'what if' or 'why couldn't' simply do not arise. In Presence, gratitude replaces misgiving as our *modus operandi*.

In Presence, we see all things as beautiful, yet Presence is anything but pollyannaish. Presence bathes reality in a beneficent light, but in Presence we also see the hard lines and jagged edges of a violent world. In Presence, we behold all without judgment, but not without discernment.

Critical thinking can easily become sclerosis for our souls. Presence dissolves the mental plaque that hardens our hearts.

Presence manifests the seminal mystery of the cosmos: death and life are not antonyms but synonyms. Presence is life in death, simultaneously and seamlessly. Presence is *necessarily* the death of the egoic self. The death of the ego is a *result* of Presence, not an act prior to Presence. Presence reveals the illusion of ego and the nothingness of death.

Presence is electric. It fills any situation with a current of spiritual aliveness. Yet it does so at a frequency that does not short-circuit us with excitement but gently illumines us with the soft light of divine love.

Presence is a divine tuning fork bringing us into perfect harmony with all that is.

Presence is filled with infinite gentleness. Presence is a consciousness more prescient than conscience. Presence is bereft of judgment, but not of wisdom. Presence delivers discernment while ending deliberation. Presence allows us to see all with the benevolent gaze of God.

Abstraction and categorization have no place in the mystery of Presence. Everything beheld in Presence is absolutely singular. It is the mystery of being that touches us in Presence.

Presence unites and differentiates simultaneously. Perfect Presence unites and differentiates perfectly.

Differentiation in Presence is something different from division, dialectic, dichotomy. It is an experience of otherness without alienation, alterity without animosity. Presence is the space in which freedom and communion flourish as non-rivalrous twins.

Joy is an infallible indicator of living in Presence. Bliss wells up spontaneously within us as, in Presence, we intuit the gratuity of being.

In Presence, we become more transparent. We become less preoccupied with self and more spontaneous with others. In Presence, there is nothing to hide because there is nothing we claim as our own.

No one in Presence would dream of pursuing holiness. The whole undertaking would seem a game and charade to them. What is there to achieve? Where is there to go? Who is there to impress?

In Presence, it's not what we do but how we do it. In Presence, how we do anything is how we do everything.

Presence is devoid of self-obsession but filled with self-awareness. Presence gives us acute situational awareness yet makes us patient with an obtuse world.

Presence holds open the space for the other without fear or expectation. Presence invites self-appreciation without expanding the ego. Presence is a space of wordless affirmation.

In Presence, we realize we do not belong to ourselves. In Presence, we experience a high degree of self-possession but always as a gift. In Presence, we recognize our own deep-down goodness and the goodness of others. We see in others the same capacity for Presence we enjoy. In Presence, we see that 'I am' and 'you are' are indivisible in the great, primordial 'I AM.'

Presence waits for the perfect word, a word that comes not from the self but from a Source beyond the self. Nothing comes forth in Presence other than what is given. Those gifted to speak from Presence do so with an authority unlike others.

It is impossible to script what comes forth in Presence. An idea, arising in Presence, gives birth to form, yet both idea and form possess the creator and are not possessed by him. No one is more aware of this than the artist to whom inspiration is given. All creative, artistic, inventive genius comes forth as a gift from Presence.

Because Presence is not stoic indifference, it grieves unconscious behavior in the same movement as it forgives it.

Presence inhabits the half-life of every instant. Presence knows the Now as an indefinable point involuting ever further, ever more deeply.

Presence expands outward even as it settles more deeply into silence. Resting in Presence, we radiate a peace beyond ourselves.

Presence functions like spiritual and social WD-40. It opens hearts that are bolted down and lubricates relationships that are stuck. Friction is eliminated wherever Presence is applied.

Presence is the space of epiphanic awareness. Insights cannot be thought, revelations cannot be created. They arrive unbidden in the intentional emptiness of Presence.

Presence precludes transactional living. There is no 'if-then' in Presence. Presence is allergic to exhortation and invective. Nothing is more alien to Presence than moralistic preaching.

Presence is inherently promissory. Devoid of pressure, Presence promises good things ahead. Presence fills us with hope. Presence is pregnant with an eschatological fullness of light, love and joy.

Presence is inherently redemptive, fastening on every failure as an opportunity for salvific self-transcendence. Presence is the practice of living consciously and kindly as the observer of our own unconscious, egoistic behavior. In Presence, even our missteps seem those of an infant learning to walk.

Presence engenders a genuine and abiding sense of humor. If, as Chesterton says, 'angels can fly because they take themselves lightly,' then so can we when practicing Presence. In Presence, life is taken seriously, but with a grain of salt added for flavor.

Presence reveals our despair, dejection and depression as negligible, unnecessary and ignorant. Presence does not bemoan our stupidity but subverts it with acceptance and good humor. Presence shows us the exit ramp to our miseries, not by boo-hooing but by poo-hooing them.

Presence does not recognize the word 'but.' As far as Presence is concerned, everything after 'but' is bullshit.

Presence never finds fault, never permits accusation. Still, Presence is acutely aware of evil as the absence of Presence.

Presence is everything, evil is no-thing. Presence refuses to make no-thing into something. Evil is the not the opposite of Presence. Presence has no equal or opposite. Evil as the absence of Presence is still nothing to be exercised about.

Presence reveals the demonic as the practice of demonization. The world of unconscious behavior is constructed upon the demonic. Presence delivers us from evil.

Presence awakens us to the performative power of language. In Presence, we realize our words are actions, not just utterances. We stop wasting our breath with anodyne speech. We witness to Presence always, using words only when necessary. When speaking in Presence, our words come forth with authority. They are alive with illocutionary power.

Presence is not something we can comprehend. Presence is a mystery that comprehends us. When we find ourselves immersed in Presence it's because Presence was somehow there before us. Awareness of our awareness discloses the priority of Presence.

Presence is like water, always seeking the deepest, darkest, lowest place with its life-giving power. Nothing penetrates more deeply than Presence. Presence buoys up and saves all that has fallen. In the absolute blackness of failure, Presence appears as a promissory light.

Immersed in Presence, we are relatively immune to the arrows and slings of this world's outrageous fortunes. 'Relatively' immune because, in Presence, we can still get our feelings hurt. But almost immediately those hurt feelings are relativized by the healing power of Presence.

Presence unleashes our imagination. In Presence, a thousand different ways present themselves to accept and manage any situation. When lost in our thoughts, we often don't know what to do or say. In Presence, solutions spontaneously suggest themselves with disarming simplicity.

In Presence, nothing seems a dead end. Instead, dead ends become occasions of grace. Waiting in stunned silence, the answer always comes through simply being present. In Presence, this advice is often given: 'Do nothing rather than something impulsive.'

In Presence, our words proclaim more than they propose, they announce more than they describe. There is a prophetic, kerygmatic power inherent in Presence. In Presence, our words and actions possess an authority missing in ordinary discourse. The difference is palpable.

Preachers or teachers would do well to spend more time cultivating Presence than analyzing texts. Words have power only to the extent they emerge from Presence. It's not the words that impact the hearer, it's the Presence with which they are spoken. Creative genius is unsurprising once we apprehend its ultimate Source as Presence.

Presence often provokes as much outrage as it inspires admiration. The collision of Presence with unconsciousness is not always a pretty picture. Sometimes it awakens more animosity than appreciation, more alienation than emulation. Presence is a two-edged sword, causing division even as it seeks to generate concord.

Presence prompts some to double-down on their obstreperousness, while others awaken to the new day promised by Presence. No promoter of Presence is welcome in the hometown of the unconscious (cf. Lk. 4:24).

In Presence, consciousness and conscience elide. In Presence, doing the right next thing becomes connatural, second-nature. To see the good, when fully present, is to do the good. Acting virtuously in Presence is the trans-rational perfection of every rational person.

With moralists, conscience sometimes acquires a bad name, retaining overtones of a harsh and demanding heteronomy. The 'you should's' overshadow the 'you can's.' True conscience is acquired through the practice of Presence. Presence never dictates, it only reveals.

In Presence, to know the good is to do the good. In Presence, it's as impossible to reject what is good as it is for a man dying of thirst in the desert to refuse to drink from an oasis. When we abide in Presence it is virtually impossible to do what is wrong or contrary to truth.

Presence is a transformative Source of love that bewilders those who think primarily in terms of right and wrong. Presence is at once the indictment and exoneration of ethical systems.

Presence is a mystery that takes us beyond good and evil. Presence is an experience of deifying beauty that issues in virtuous behavior almost as an afterthought.

Presence is a swirling river of inspirational cross-currents. In Presence, we are moved this way and that, never stagnating in thought, always carried forward in hope. In Presence, everything is made new at every moment. In Presence, the lightness of being seems unbearable.

Once we have come to trust the power of Presence to transform any situation from darkness into light, we seek to return to Presence as often as possible. Sanctity is remaining as continuously present as is humanly possible.

Familiarity with Presence is such that even our falls from Presence precipitate our immediate return. Life in Presence is a constant dynamic of redemptive awareness.

Presence is the path to joy, and joy is the fruit of Presence.

Placing any person or situation in Presence bathes them in a supernal light of infinite blessing. Nothing has changed yet everything is different. In Presence, a transcendental perspective arises that affords promise and hope in the direst of circumstances.

Presence proves itself a jealous lover. It commands, without demanding. It requires our undivided attention and issues in our unconditional surrender. When we give ourselves over to Presence, it gives everything to us. Those who love Presence discover the real meaning of love.

Presence is 'the pearl of great price' (Mt. 13:46). Though buried in plain sight, it is difficult to find but impossible to forget. We would give everything to possess it, only to discover that it already possesses us.

Presence is a sacrament of holy communion in which otherness and union meet, freedom and love kiss. Presence is a nuptial mystery of unity and diversity in which we can be different without division and united without identification.

Presence is the sacred space of eternal allowing in which alterity flourishes and alienation is unknown. Presence is an arena of acceptance where distinctions stand out but divorce does not occur. Presence is the paradise where 'the lion and lamb' learn to live together in love (cf. Isa. 11:6-7).

Nothing is forced in Presence. Presence involves an attentiveness that is at once effortful and effortless. In Presence, we remain open yet empty, alert but relaxed. Presence is the space of pure gift. All is given in Presence according to the openness of the receiver.

Even if the concept of God can no longer do so, Presence remains undiminished it is power to communicate a why-less love.

Presence disarms and subverts what is wrong, it doesn't correct it. Confrontation is out of place in Presence. Presence overcomes resistance with acceptance, rebellion with release.

Presence conforms to the prickly objects it receives like space in a room or water in a lake. It dissolves what is harsh or hard without opposing it. In Presence, there are no head-on collisions. Whatever has gone awry is made right again in an ocean of gentleness, not in a whirlwind of might.

In Presence, we remain unperturbed but not indifferent. Presence sharpens our moral and aesthetic senses, while sublating them within a higher, accepting, forgiving love. Presence is a space of infinite peace and a bottomless depth of empathy and compassion.

Presence reveals compassion not primarily as an ethical good but as an ontological given. Presence manifests a Source of benevolence beyond our genealogy of morals. There is something primordially awe-full about Presence, of which 'being good' is a poor facsimile.

Grim determination finds no purchase in Presence. Presence is a flow, effort is a grind. One moment of Presence is worth more than a lifetime of resolute will.

Everything touched by Presence is instantly redeemed. The kindly light of Presence softens the hardest stare, melts the stoniest heart. No created power can forever resist the liquifying power of Presence. In the end, Presence will be 'all in all' (cf. 1 Cor. 15:28).

Presence is a purgatory of grief and a paradise of gratitude. In Presence, we grieve the violence of the world and rejoice at being immersed in an ocean of love.

Presence inclines us more and more to silence. In Presence, we are loathe to utter a cliché or unconsciously opine. Presence reminds us of our mothers' motto: 'If you have nothing good to say, say nothing at all.'

Presence sees no evil, speaks no evil, does no evil. Those who abide in Presence 'abide in love' (cf. 1 Jn. 4:16).

Presence is the alchemical crucible in which our hearts of lead are turned to hearts of gold. Presence is the purifying fire in which our ego is melted down and our true self appears.

Presence is the place of our deification. A saint's halo is a nimbus of Presence.

Presence backlights the lives of those given over to it. In Presence, the corona of love becomes palpable. Presence beatifies those possessed of it.

Presence is an invisible mesh that makes humanity a seamless whole. Presence is also the indefinable power that makes possible our conscious connection with nature. "I said to the almond tree, 'Sister, speak to me of God.' And the almond tree blossomed."[11]

---

[11] Nikos Kazantzakis, *Report to Greco.*

In Presence, all things appear as gift. Presence is the space in which we allow reality to 'present itself' on its own terms.

Presence is the space where alterity is permitted and otherness shines forth in irreducible and irreplaceable beauty. Presence is the space where alienation and opposition are unknown. In Presence, every concrete singular presents itself as a 'present,' as a gift.

Presence disabuses us of our *need* to help others. There is no compulsivity in Presence, including that of running to someone's rescue. In Presence, we recognize the power of healing or of helping comes not *from* us but *through* us. Compassion is communicated only through Presence, even where technical assistance is required. Presence is the death of altruism but the lifeblood of emphatic love.

Presence accommodates an out-of-control person like a matador stepping aside to defeat a raging bull. Craziness exhausts itself in the arena of Presence.

The purpose of a koan is to point us to Presence. Presence is the sound of one hand clapping. Presence is the face we had before we were born.

Presence is a space of innocent perception. In Presence, our vision is continually refreshed. We see with the eyes of a child but with the wisdom of a sage.

All is intuitively known in Presence. Objects are seen as sacramental expressions of an excess of being. Creation itself appears miraculous. In Presence, awe and wonder replace worry and anxiety. A fundamental okness about life pervades the space of Presence.

Thoughts assault Presence like soldiers an enemy fortress. They are easily dispatched if our moat of awareness is expansive enough.

Presence gives us an acute anticipation of we-know-not-what. In Presence, we intuit an implicit fullness (*plērōma*) that brings us continuous joy. Presence is the space in which hope springs eternal.

In Presence, we are aware of our moods and transcend them. Presence allows us to experience our emotional fluctuations while at the same time sublating them in an ocean of benign acceptance.

In Presence, our emotional inconstancy is acknowledged and overcome. In Presence, we experience the strength that comes from recognizing our weaknesses and simply leaving them alone.

We experience the power of Presence to a more or less degree depending on the deliberateness with which we give ourselves over to it. Presence is the tacit Source of illumination of everything we see, but when it becomes the explicit focus of our attention, Presence possesses us in a divinizing way.

In Presence, we experience a certain ecstasy about the is-ness of things. In Presence, we delight in the beauty of the present moment. In Presence, everything seems perfect by virtue of the sheer fact of its here-and-now-ness. Presence is an intuition of being that brings infinite bliss.

In Presence, we *belong* to that which we *behold*. In Presence, we welcome what is different from ourselves and make room in ourselves for it in ourselves. In giving ourselves over to that which presents itself, we acknowledge our belongingness with all that comes our way. Presence is an experience of communion with all that is other from us.

Presence calls us to ever-greater simplicity. Presence beckons us to ever-deeper silence. In Presence, stillness speaks. In Presence, our attentiveness is as acute as our expectations are absent. In Presence, we are reduced to a still-point of infinite openness. In Presence, egoic poverty is spiritual fecundity.

We enter Presence like storybook characters entering a secret passage. Susan and Edmund discover nothing in Narnia[12] as enchanting and transforming as what we find in Presence.

Devoid of expectations, Presence is also the end of resentment. Expectations are premeditated resentments. Lose the expectations, lose the resentments. Practice Presence, enjoy peace.

---

[12] C. S. Lewis, *The Lion, the Witch and the Wardrobe.*

Ego dissolves in Presence. The moment we become fully present, ego evaporates. Self-forgetfulness, though not self-awareness, takes its place. Completely attentive to the other, we become as nothing, yet we feel more fulfilled than ever. In Presence, death to self is newness of life.

Presence is an experience of ever-deeper relinquishment, of ever-more-complete letting go. Relaxing into Presence is a bottomless adventure. Here, surrender is victory, self-forgetfulness is self-discovery. In Presence, we experience the paradox of self-emptying as self-fulfillment.

Presence is not the dissolution of self, only of ego. Ego is our ersatz identity. Our true identity is experienced in Presence, yet we cannot grasp this identity any more than we can catch our shadow or see our eyes without a mirror.

In Presence, the other's joy is our joy, the other's sorrow our sorrow. Presence is an ethos of empathy minus pathos. Presence is perfect compassion without condescension.

Presence communicates confidence. When listening in Presence, we gain a sense of the worthwhile-ness of every aspect of life. Listening to others in Presence, we become humble and grateful.

A person in Presence is like a mother listening to her infant's baby monitor, but without anxiety. It is an expectant openness suffused with love.

It is impossible to listen carefully and be thinking at the same time. Presence necessarily suspends thought. Within this pause of being present, love and wisdom unite.

Presence is the place of ego-less self-possession. We are never more in control of ourselves than when in Presence, yet never less occupied with ourselves. In Presence, self-awareness and self-appreciation expand, self-interest and self-obsession recede.

Presence is a space of relaxed attentiveness. It's a place of intentional unknowing, a place in which the other is allowed to be seen, as if for the first time. Presence is the place of no agenda, no expectations, no preconceptions. Presence is the place of surprise where nothing, and everything, is always new.

Presence is a soft afternoon light burnishing our lives with a supernal beauty. Presence is the benign smile of a grandfather watching his grandchildren play. Presence is the dying of the wind, allowing the sound to carry across the waters of our souls.

In Presence, we awaken to the miracle of being. We intuit a deep-down freshness. In Presence, we receive a proleptic sense of the plērōmic fullness that our temporal existence portends. Presence is filled with unnameable promise.

Presence is an eschatological awareness. It is a sense that the fullness of time has already arrived and is yet to come. Presence is a pregnant expectation of we-know-not-what.

Presence is the space of for-giveness. In Presence, beneficent attention is 'given' to the other before it is requested. Presence is, as it were, love paid forward in the form of unrestricted, non-judgmental openness to the other. Presence is the space of grace-filled acceptance.

Presence is the space of poise and repose. Presence is where *kairos* redeems *chronos*, where 'timing is everything' and 'time means nothing.' Presence is where we don't move until we see it; where we are neither too early nor too late. Presence is the place where the maxim, 'God's timing is always perfect' comes true.

To discover Presence is the spiritual equivalent of the mathematical discovery of zero. Nothing in itself, Presence infuses meaning into all the moments that are counted as time.

Presence is as undefinable and indivisible as the apex of an arching arrow or a ball tossed in the air. Presence is akin to the point of zero gravity at the epicenter of a teeter-totter. Presence can be experienced in the virginal point at the deepest center of who we are - the *Le Point Vierge* - where our humanity and the Mystery of divinity intersect.[13]

---

[13] See above, n. 2.

Presence penetrates, permeates, and renders totally transparent those who give themselves over to it. Presence suffuses us as light a crystal clear window, or fire an incandescent log. Presence is the means of our 'divinization.'[14]

The transfiguring effect of Presence is altogether unrelated to the moral or ethical condition of the person who is present. Presence is the immediate dissolution of our sins. In Presence, we instantly rise above whatever depths of deprivation our personal lives may have fallen into.

Presence is the space in which we stand back from ourselves in a separation of salvific bliss. Presence is perspective on all that is problematic in ourselves and in the rest of the world. In the perspective Presence provides, peace arises. In Presence, all is calm, all is bright.

Would that a critical mass of humanity awaken to the mystery of Presence! Such would be an apocalyptic event worth waiting for.

In Presence, questions about God's wisdom do not arise. No one in Presence ever asks: 'Why does God allow so much suffering?' or 'Why doesn't God do something about the world situation?'. Presence reveals such questions as so much silliness. Presence shows the God behind such questions to be nothing other than a Wizard of Oz.

---

[14] See St. John of the Cross, *The Ascent of Mount Carmel, II, 5, 6; The Living Flame of Love, I, 4, 19-24*. Also, St. Athanasius, *On the Incarnation, 54*.

Presence is the bubble wrap in which our fragile world is cushioned. Wrapped in Presence, we have less chance of breaking.

Presence is the place where God relieves us of our fears, doubts and insecurities. In Presence, our questions, expectations, resentments and pre-judgments are taken away. In the space of the absolute Now, shame and guilt about the past and anxiety and worry about the future find no foothold. In Presence, we become poor in spirit but are spiritually enriched. In Presence, we are emptied of our attachments but filled with God's life.

Our lives are 'hidden with God' in Presence (cf. Col. 3:3). Our true identity is disclosed to us - and then only dimly - when we are immersed in Presence. Only God knows our real names when we abide in Presence.

Patience and Presence are synonymous. In Presence, we have nowhere to go and nowhere to be than where we are right here, right now.

Presence is the end of rushing around. Nothing is hurried when we abide in Presence. Those we encounter when we practice Presence never feel they are interrupting. Instead, they experience us as having all the time in the world. And they would be right.

Presence is contagious. Presence radiates out from us like an electro-magnetic field. Everyone we encounter in Presence feels its pull. When we abide in Presence, others experience us as a breath of fresh air, a wave of divine mercy, a manifestation of unconditional love.

Knowing Presence is like knowing our guardian angel. Presence is a power greater than ourselves, inseparable from us at all times and in all places, ever ready to rescue us from the sufferings caused by our falls into unconscious, egoic action, pulling us back into the light when we have gotten lost in the darkness.

Presence is the true mount of beatitude. There we realize how blessed we are to be poor in spirit. We feel the kingdom of heaven is ours. In Presence, we are comforted even in our mourning. We are filled with a hunger and thirst for doing what is right. We are suffused with mercy and realize this is God's mercy towards us. We desire nothing other than to be peacemakers and so to be called children of God. We even receive the inspiration to love our enemies and bless those who criticize or condemn us. In Presence, everything is pure joy, a participation in divine beatitude (cf. Mt. 5:3-12).

The heart keeps nothing for itself but pumping lifeblood to the body. Presence is the heart of our identity in God, pumping divine lifeblood into us for the transfiguration of our bodies, minds, souls and spirits.

Holiness means marinating in Presence. Sanctity means being saturated with Presence.

Deification is a dyeing process. In Presence, the fabric of our lives is empurpled with God's divinity.

We can consent to, but not compel, the advent of Presence. Presence is at once a gift and a task, something we fundamentally are and something we need to acquire. The very desire to be more present is itself Presence 'coming like a thief in the night' to awaken us to a better way of living (cf. Mt. 24:43).

Presence shushes the kerfuffle. Presence is a no kerfluffling zone. Histrionics are silenced by Presence.

True authority, unassuming yet commanding, issues automatically in Presence. Speaking or acting from Presence communicates a gravitas that cannot but be noticed by others. Real authority has nothing to do with status or office; it has everything to do with the degree of Presence that a person speaks or acts.

Presence is infinitely gentle, even when it commands our attention or silences our ego. Those who abide in Presence speak and act with authority, yet their words and actions invite others to join them in a place of respectful responsibility and kindly understanding. Presence is always a person-to-person connection, summoning the other to awaken to Presence.

Presence is an inner light leading us through the darkest neighborhoods in our inner and outer worlds. Presence gives us hope in the valley of death and gives us joy amidst the slings and arrows of life.

Presence allows us to remain self-possessed even when we notice ourselves becoming afraid or panicked. Presence burns like a pilot light within - not even the harsh winds of the world's tempests can extinguish it. Presence is the candle in our inner lighthouse, guiding us to safe harbor when we feel lost at sea.

Presence is inextinguishable since it is at the Source of our very existence as rational, conscious creatures. No amount of egoic facade can damage or destroy our underlying original beauty as self-transcendently conscious creatures. No matter what happens to us, not matter what we have done or what the consequences of our actions, the moment all is placed in Presence, all is forgiven, all is redeemed.

Acknowledgement of our mistakes is already to have risen above them. Noticing our masks of ego is momentarily to have shed them. The challenge is to live in the space of acknowledgement, to abide in the place of mask-less-ness.

Practicing Presence, we need only to walk around to beautify the world and give hope to the hopeless. No amount of altruistic social work does as much good at a stroll in the park when we are practicing Presence.

Presence possesses us, never us it. Presence is a power greater than ourselves in which we discover our true selves. In Presence, we realize every identity we have constructed for ourselves outside of Presence is false. In Presence, we realize that all we have said or done apart from Presence is, in some sense, fraudulent. At the same time, we become aware that one word, one act, performed while fully present, outweighs in pure gold all the lead ingots we have placed on the other half of the scale. Discovering Presence, whether for the first time or again and again, is always an experience of redeeming joy.

Presence is purgatory and heaven wrapped up as one. Presence reveals our egoic missteps in its blinding light of merciful judgment, then purifies our hearts by making us increasingly aware of when we are departing from Presence. Ultimately Presence makes us desire nothing but Presence, so great is our joy and peace when abiding in Presence. Every time we enter Presence, we enter the kingdom of God. Why, once we have tasted its delights, would we ever choose to leave?

Entering Presence is like having a Near Death Experience (NDE). There is an instantaneous dissolution of the ego together with an immediately enhanced sense of personal identity. We experience ourselves as immersed in an ocean of infinite love, while at the same time knowing ourselves to be distinct from the love that suffuses us. We wish the experience never to end, yet inevitably find ourselves back in the workaday world, now aware that our practice of Presence is to be our *modus operandi* and our primary way of showing others the meaning of life.

The experience of Presence banishes our remorse about the past and our worries about the future. In Presence, we apprehend a light-filled *plērōma* (fullness) 'which no eye can see and no ear can hear' (cf. 1 Cor. 2:9).

The hope generated in Presence is unintelligible to the clever and wise of this world. It is experienced only by those, reborn as children in Presence, who have risen above the politics of the day.

Presence gives us a newfound and humble sense of our own limitations. Presence shows us intuitively how to stay in our own lane.

In Presence, we lose our need to perform, pretend, or overreach. In Presence, we know that less is generally more.

In Presence, we discover our true strengths and weaknesses, preferences and aversions with neither shame, nor guilt, neither pride nor apology. Presence is a place of perfect contentment, a place where we delight as much in our deficiencies as in our abilities.

In Presence, we feel it's impossible to make a mistake. In Presence, we glimpse our freedom as the absence of our need to decide. Keeping our options open seems unnecessary. In Presence, we intuitively know how to handle things that used to baffle us.

In Presence, we sense the perfection of every present moment, even in its apparently senselessness. Presence saves us from carping about anything or anyone. Presence takes us to a place where we know beyond a doubt, that 'all will be well, and all manner of things will be well.'[15]

Presence wears the knowing smile of a Cheshire cat.

Relaxing into the nadir of surrender, we are borne on eagle's wings into the kingdom of God. Descending into the infinite depths of acceptance (*Gelassenheit*, letting go), we ascend into heaven.

Presence is the end of our desire to exercise control. In Presence, we make no attempt to resist the currents of life, nor push the bus we are riding in.

---

[15] See above, n. 3.

Presence reveals death and life as the selfsame mystery.

Presence explodes our attempts to give it expression. In Presence, we preach without using words. For those gifted to speak about Presence, what is given in Presence outruns and strains to the breaking point their capacity to do so. Anyone who speaks or acts in Presence does so with the greatest of ease and peace.

Presence may be practiced but never possessed. Presence requires cooperation, but cannot be commanded. Presence is an act of letting go, in which our surrender of ego is immediate and complete. Attempts to break attachments to attain Presence are but a doubling-down on ego. It's just as easy to become attached to detachment as to anything else. Detachment is more a result of our awakening to Presence than a requirement for entering it.

In Presence, we are drawn, as if by magnetic force, into a vanishing point of eternal illumination. We are pulled into a vortex of belongingness that opens unto universal love.

Presence is the soft light of a mid-October late afternoon, beautifying all that is dying. There is nothing harsh about the dying light of Presence. Everything looks beautiful in Presence, including death itself.

In Presence, we neither fear nor anticipate death. Presence is already death to self, so what is there to fear? Presence dissolves every false identity, allowing our hearts and souls to rise from the tomb of the artificial ego.

Presence is a theophanic event. In Presence, a person becomes like the burning bush in the desert, consumed but not destroyed, made incandescent by an interior noumenosity that is both attractive and disarming to those who behold it (cf. Ex. 3:2-6).

Athletes who perform with Presence describe the game 'as coming to them' or as 'slowing down.' They see, as if in slow motion, what, for other, more frenetic athletes, seems a blur. They play in complete possession of themselves. They also perform with a *joie-de-vivre* not possible for those who are 'just grinding it out.'

Presence defeats evil without ever resisting it. Presence recognizes evil for the puffed up illusion it is.

Presence is the space where bluster and blather dissipate. Presence is the place where pride and presumption peter out. Presence stands over the corpse of sin like David over the body of Goliath, but without ever having thrown a stone or fired a shot.

Presence illumines only the next step, the next breath, the next stroke of the broom, the next right thing. Presence is God's kindly light giving us only enough clarity to move ahead slowly. Presence keeps from getting ahead of ourselves, from getting in our own way, from stumbling. And even when we stumble, Presence immediately shows us the way up and out of the difficulty.

Presence is a no politics zone. Presence silences political debate without ever speaking a word. Presence judges no one, yet shows political wrangling to be a waste of time.

Presence is God's alternative to society's insanity. Presence is God's offer of escape from the world's coo-coo's nest.

In Presence, we are not trying to get somewhere or achieve something. Presence is its own destination and its own reward. Self-fulfillment is the happy by-product of the vanishing of self that occurs automatically the moment we become present.

Meditation and practicing Presence are synonymous. Meditation becomes artificial when it attains to anything other than deepening our felt-sense of the infinite depths of the present moment.

There is an *immediacy* in Presence that defies our ability to articulate. Presence escapes our capacity to fully experience it, even when we are completely present. In Presence, it's as if we are perpetually chasing a Light beckoning us into a deeper abyss of the present moment.

There is a *plērōma* of Presence that forever eludes us. Presence is a Power greater than ourselves, while at the same time, the immediate Source and Satisfaction of our conscious existence.

Presence is the virginal space in which those with no religious affiliation or inclination can find satisfaction for their spiritual desires. Presence shows the true a-theist and the true believer to be in pursuit and possession of the same Mystery. Presence makes friends of believers and unbelievers in an experience of transcendental oneness.

Presence affirms what mystics of all religious traditions have told us - to apprehend the Mystery of God, we must go beyond and even discard our concepts of God. We must become a-theistic to experience the Reality to which our theistic beliefs point.

Presence is an experience of satiation and saturation. Presence is a saturated event - something so rich, so dense that our inward gaze cannot bear it. This weight of Presence is not an unhappiness or a grief but an excess of joy and awe. The weight of Presence is 'the weight of glory' (cf. 2 Cor. 4:17).

Presence is a treasure buried in plain sight. Everyone is capable of being fully present, but very few are, relatively speaking. The world is in the mess it is, not for want of intelligence but for a lack of Presence. Unawakened persons are like those looking for the glasses perched on their heads.

Presence reveals much of what passes as intelligence to be learned ignorance and aggrandized imbecility. The peace of Presence is inaccessible to the questioning intellect. Yet, intellectual inquiry that questions its own ultimacy opens out onto Presence and is sometimes its own redemption.

Presence is infinite awareness and awareness of the Infinite. Intellection is finite analysis and analysis of the finite. Presence is the precondition for the possibility of cognition, not an object or outcome of cognition. Presence arises when cognition awakens to the limits of its own activity and dimly apprehends the Source of its limited powers.

The humility of intellectuals who apprehend the ontological priority of Presence is more inspiring than whatever works their collective genius may produce.

Presence is the invisible penumbra accompanying every beautiful or inspiring thought. Thought, if it awakens to an awareness of itself, will glimpse this glorious nimbus.

Living in Presence, we move through life as fish in a school, or birds in a flock. They move as one, turning this way and that, without deliberate willing or doing but with an intuitive knowing not given to those not living in Presence. Those unfamiliar with Presence move through life as though in a perpetual traffic jam, angry and frustrated that the flow is not what they expected.

One moment of Presence releases more glory into the cosmos than all empires come and gone in history.

Presence is activated with the appearance of the other. Turning our attention to another, we either bathe them in the divine light of Presence or cast them into the outer darkness of our uninterested, objectifying stare.

Presence is our unbreakable connection with every person we encounter. Presence is an invisible umbilical cord that fastens us, at every instant, with the Source of life and with the whole of humanity.

Presence is a permanently pentecostal, theophanic light. Presence always appears as an epiphany, yet abides unchangingly as the divine dimension of every person.

Only a humanity that is always already divine can manifest Presence.

Presence flashes forth from unconsciousness like Christ from the tomb. Presence is a taste of the resurrection for those who have rejected the Christian gospel.

Presence fills the present moment with such an excess of joy as to portend a future fullness (*plērōma*) of Presence unconditioned by time and space.

Presence is an experience of perpetual surprise. Presence seems miraculous every time it arises within us. Presence never fails to engender a fresh sense of gratitude for the gift of being. Presence is a reconstitution and perfection of our original state of innocence.

Presence allows us to hear the silence speak. Presence reveals silence as the small, still voice of God (cf. 1 Kg. 19:2).

Presence relieves us of the need to speak of God. In Presence, we realize that not speaking of God, at least as a noun, may be the most honorable way of respecting both God's transcendence and immanence.

Presence allows us to perceive egregious injustices and social animosities without becoming one with them by passing judgment upon them. In Presence, we learn the subtle but salvific distinction between empathetically observing and critically reacting.

Acting to achieve social justice apart from the experience of Presence is futile. Only the viscosity of Presence allows the gears of justice to move smoothly. Otherwise our systems of justice become meat grinders, tearing to shreds both advocates and accused.

For those practicing Presence, no preparation is necessary. For those who do not, no preparation is sufficient.

When, in Presence, we let go of our concepts of God, we experience God's Presence in our act of letting go.

Presence is the loss of every identifiable sense of self, while at the same time an intuition of our transcendental identity in God. In Presence, we glimpse ourselves as we are known by God (cf. 1 Cor. 13:12).

Presence fills the unbridgeable hiatus between creation and Creator, between all that exists and its ungenerated Source. Presence is the sophianic ethos within which the Infinite permeates the finite, and the finite partakes of the Infinite.

Presence reveals politics to be so much pettifoggery. Presence rescues us from the debates and dialectics of an antinimous social order. Presence delivers us from the hellish consequences of imitative rivalries.

Presence is both gift and task. We must make the effort to 'be present,' yet, in Presence, we realize that our awakening to Presence is always a gift. In Presence, we experience everything as a gift, yet living consciously in Presence requires intentionality.

Presence is holding the space for the other to be other. Presence is the space of intentional allowing. Presence buffers us from insult while allowing those who insult to blow off steam.

Presence is the place of the perpetual smile, devoid of patronization. Presence is the benevolent light in which there is no shadow of misgiving.

Presence defeats demonization and silences the clamor for a scapegoat. Presence is the space of complete accountability and complete acceptance. Presence is the space where complete understanding leads to complete forgiveness.

Presence both reveals and dissolves our smallest and largest character defects. Presence functions both as a sin detector and a sin transformer. In Presence, our wounds become our badges of honor, our sins revealed as the backside of a beautiful tapestry.

Speak to a child in Presence and they hang on every word. Even infants in the womb respond knowingly to words spoken to them in Presence.

Presence makes us increasingly sensitive to the egregious sins of condescension and patronization, as in Presence there is no room for either the smirk or the shrug. At the same time, Presence echoes the prayer 'but for the grace of God, there go I.' Presence is the glass house in which no stone throwing is allowed.

Presence is a space of poised relaxation, of powerful softness. In Presence, we remain alert but not alarmed, aware but not naive. Presence is the space in which we accept what is in light of what we know can be.

In Presence, indictment and exoneration are synonymous but not indistinguishable. Presence renders evil irrelevant but no less tragic. Presence is absent pathos but not patience.

Thoughts and emotions appear and disappear in Presence as randomly and unpredictably as neutrinos in a vacuum. Phenomena disappear in a pool of Presence like pebbles in a pond, but without ripple or sound.

Presence is what makes ego-less self-love possible. In Presence, everything and everyone is lovable, including (especially?) oneself.

Presence is an experience of realized eschatology - an acute yet diffused anticipation of a future that has already arrived, save in its ultimate fullness (*plērōma*).

A person consciously practicing Presence - i.e., being as present as possible every possible moment - beautifies the world simply by walking around. Others are healed just by her passing by.

Presence is time out of time. It's the conflation of *kairos* (timing) with *chronos* (clock time). Presence touches a child's heart when they first hear those enchanting words, 'Once upon a time...'

Presence is the androgynous Mystery in which the silent, strong Joseph invisibly supports the unspeakably merciful Mary to give birth to children of God. In the silent night of Presence, all is calm, all is bright. In Presence, every moment is Christmas.

Rules and regulations - laws - are needed where Presence is missing. When Presence arises, however, no iron fist is needed to keep people in line.

Presence has built into it an understanding that 'But for the grace of God, there go I.' Nevertheless, in Presence, punitive talk and actions feel like fingernails on the blackboard.

The grief of the ego is the bliss of the spirit. Suffering subverts itself. When the pain of holding on becomes greater than the pain of letting go, we let go. Presence arises when our egoic somnambulism collides with reality.

In Presence, diminishment and death are just as perfect and beautiful as the birth of a baby. Autumn is not the obverse of Spring, nor winter the opposite of summer. Presence delights in the kaleidoscope of nature with every changing moment.

Presence is hospice for the cancerous ego. As the ego consumes itself with tumors of drama, sarcasm and self-pity, Presence sits invisibly near-by waiting for the struggling to stop. When it does, the Light of eternity appears.

Presence is the loving parent helping us out of the Halloween costumes of our ego.

Only in Presence do we discover our own voice, our own true faces. The deeper we move into Presence, the less duplicitous, even by omission, we become. At the same time, the freedom found in Presence is such that scrupulosity also disappears.

In Presence, every person appears as *sui generis*, one of a kind.

Writing or speaking of Presence must be an epiphanic event, otherwise it loses the existential immediacy of what it purports to describe. We should speak of Presence only when caught up in Presence. Only when we are gifted with an eruption of Presence should we attempt to give it expression.

Presence, when manifest, is always something of a surprise, a welcome respite from the tedium of unconscious living, a blessed oasis in the desert of intellection, analysis and argumentation.

Presence is an apocalypse, an unveiling, a pulling back of the curtain between time and eternity. Presence is the eruption of the Infinite in the finite, the appearance of the Ineffable amidst the fallible. Presence always inspires awe and gratitude. Presence is always experienced as a blessing from beyond.

Presence separates the trivial many from the vital few. Indeed, only one thing is necessary - mindfulness in every moment.

Presence is the space in which things emerge and unfold organically. Presence has an earthly, i.e., 'down-to-earth' humility (humus) about it. Presence compels us not to rush, not to expect to produce fruit quickly from the seeds of contemplation we plant in our hearts by practicing Presence. Presence generates within us the patience of the farmer who knows that there is a season and a cycle for everything, and that all things come to harvest only when the time is ripe.

Presence frees us to acknowledge our mistakes. In Presence, the sweet pledge of a blessed future dissolves the bitter aftertaste of past failures. In Presence, we are happy to 'boast of our weaknesses' (cf. 2 Cor. 11:30; 12:9), now that the promise of new beginnings is so palpable.

Presence allows us to listen to many voices without feeling we are at the tower of Babel. Presence is that liminal space in which all voices can be listened to without judgment, without confusion, without comparison.

Presence allows us to suspect a transcendent symphony where other might hear only racket. Presence is that anagogical space in which a glorious end, yet to be revealed, promises a beatific, harmonious chorus of praise.

Presence strips us of our codependent enmeshment with others, while opening us more fully to every 'other'. We are never more - or less - alone than when in Presence. In Presence, we experience ourselves and others as beautifully irreplaceable and unsubstitutable. We also experience our uniqueness as constitutive of our communion.

Presence allows us to bump up against the limits of our understanding without continuing to bang our heads against those walls. We no longer need to chip away, like wannabe escapees, at the prison bars of our own understanding. In Presence, we experience peace and joy 'beyond understanding' (cf. Phil. 4:7).

Presence is the space of true prayer, the prayer of a listening heart. When we listen to the other - whether to God or simply another person - we open ourselves to the Infinite. Presence is prayer in its most simplified form.

Presence and contemplation are, at bottom, the same. Both are a beholding without preconception or interpretation. Both are an exercise in *Gelassenheit* - letting-be - within which the other is allowed to manifest itself in an endless disclosure of its infinite depths.

Presence allows the excess of Being to show itself in any person or any object. In Presence, we realize that neither ourselves nor the person or object we behold, is the source of its own existence. The miraculous surfeit of being is intuitively felt in Presence.

Everything tastes better, and everything slows down, in Presence. Presence is the place of savoring. Nothing is rushed, all is enjoyed. When we occupy the space of Presence, even blustery, rainy days disclose an inherent beauty.

Presence is to thinking what dining is to eating. Presence is attending Babette's Feast, thinking is driving through McDonald's.[16]

Presence is the power of gentle vivification. In Presence, the contours of reality are sharpened, while the rough edges are smoothed away.

---

[16] *Babette's Feast* (Danish: *Babettes Gæstebud*) is a 1987 Danish drama film directed by Gabriel Axel.

Presence resembles the paradisal state in which we are, spiritually speaking, 'naked without shame' (cf. Gen. 2:25). The moment we enter Presence, we lose our egoic clothing and stand unabashed before the other.

Presence is an invisible black light that instantly reveals the smallest speck of ego. Even here, however, Presence illumines only to awaken. Presence brings our sins to light only to summon us into the bliss of acceptance.

Presence gives us back our spiritual virginity every time we have prostituted ourselves with unconscious living. In Presence, we become again as little children, fit for the kingdom of God (cf. Lk., 18:16). In Presence, we receive a new share of our original innocence.

In Presence, we give ourselves time to digest whatever comes our way. Presence is the place of acceptance in which things are allowed to gestate, to unfold as they will, not as we might have them.

Every moment we spend in Presence redounds to our deification and the transfiguration of the cosmos.

In Presence, penetrating to the virginal point at the deepest center of our being, we release a stream of living water that surges upward and outward, irrigating and fructifying us and the whole of creation in its heavenly ascent.

Presence is a *kenosis* that is also an *apotheosis*, a releasement that is also a resurrection, a letting go that is also a being lifted up. In Presence, we discover that death (i.e., relinquishment) is life and that the meaning of life is to loosen our death grip on it.

When we practice Presence we serve as God's air fresheners in the world. We emit a spiritual fragrance that works better than Febreze.

Presence is what allows us to move smoothly in the world - a kind of spiritual viscosity that reduces the friction wherever it is applied.

Presence is a spiritual cornucopia of wisdom and love. All good things pour forth from Presence in an unending variety of gifts for which we are truly grateful.

Presence is escape from the world of reactivity. Our mirror neurons cease to operate when we abide in Presence. In Presence, we are attuned to a kind of silent music that keeps us from listening to old mental tapes.

Presence is not the opposite of thinking; rather, it is the invisible horizon within which thinking takes place. Presence is not the opposite of anything. Presence is the space in which opposing anything appears as insane and unreal.

In Presence, we rise above all in-fighting but not without compassion for the combatants. Presence is an experience of redemptive transcendence containing no condescension.

The grammar of 'if' is unknown in Presence. In Presence, conditionality does not exist. In Presence, we make contact with the Unconditioned, making the logic of 'if-then' irrelevant.

Questions of right and wrong are more ignored than resolved in Presence. Presence looks past morality in its apprehension of a more immanent, unalloyed goodness, much like the forgiving father looks past the missteps of his prodigal son (cf. Lk. 15:11-32). Immersed in this infinite goodness, we find ourselves incapable and uninterested in making binary judgments.

Presence is an experience of being grasped and awakened by the power of the Now. It's as if we have found the magic door that is an exit from the past and future and an entrance into something that is both immediate and everlasting.

Presence is a retreat for which we never have to leave home, a retreat from our egoic selves. In Presence, we step back from ourselves as unconscious automatons and discover ourselves as intentional, self-conscious actors. Self-consciousness is synonymous with self-transcendence, and self-transcendence is the space of Presence within us where we can co-exist with others in non-reactive respect and harmony.

Presence is a diffused awareness within which everything we see, including ourselves, comes into sharper and sharper focus. Presence is the QLED background light of our lives that makes the bright spots bright in our lives brighter, and the dark spots darker. All appears perfectly beautiful within this horizon of infinite enhancement.

In Presence, we look upon the character of ourselves and others, not only with understanding and forgiveness, but also with an element of bliss, knowing that for them, as for ourselves, every unconscious misstep, every addictive habit, is an opportunity to awaken. In Presence, we realize that our greatest sin is our easiest avenue to redemption.

In the beginning, the experience of Presence may be episodic, inconsistent, easily lost. Soon, however, the awareness that we have stepped out of Presence and back into egoic insanity re-awakens us to Presence. Eventually, practicing Presence becomes our default position, making it less and less desirable to abide anywhere else.

Like an invisible, alchemical power, Presence is always at work to transmute the leaden materials of our egoic selves into pure gold. The power of Presence is such that every departure from Presence brings problems, the pain of which helps return us to Presence. Ultimately, unconsciousness is its own worst enemy.

Presence is the tacit, transcendental background in which even our self-conscious actions appear. It is impossible to live continuously, consciously in Presence. Trying to make Presence the object of our focal attention simply constellates a more primordially tacit horizon of Presence. It is always possible for us to step beyond ourselves one step further. We can look at ourselves, and then look at ourselves looking at ourselves, *ad infinitum.* Abiding in Presence means enjoying the transcendental immanence of Presence without trying to capture it.

Presence functions like a diamond-tipped drill boring swiftly and inexorably through the bedrock of our hard hearts, revealing the most sacred chamber of our being where the crystalline gold of our true identity lies.

Presence is a power that disarms, never debates; subverts, doesn't oppose. Presence is asymmetrical with everything that militates against it. Presence is the power of re-framing. In Presence, we stand apart from our problems, placing them in an ever-widening horizon of understanding and acceptance, depriving even the most vexing problems of their power to undo us.

Presence not only relativizes the problems placed within it, it also neutralizes the guilt and shame attending our mistakes. In Presence, spilled milk is quickly wiped up. In Presence, we recognize our imperfections clearly and accept them as invitations to deeper and more complete acceptance. In Presence, failure is an occasion for faith, error an opportunity for awakening.

In Presence, we are in the world but not of it (cf. Jn. 15:19).

Presence is a virginal space pregnant with divine life. Presence is a fecund womb of silence in which the surfeit of being is seen. Presence is a space where we are given a glimpse of pure actuality. In Presence, we realize it is very, very good just to be.

Prayer and Presence are, at some level, identical. Both are unrestricted openness to the Infinite. Both are complete receptivity, devoid of agenda, yet expectant of blissful satisfaction.

In Presence, we are like distant stars shining, twinkling in the night sky. We illumine and inspire - visible proof that no depth of darkness can overcome the light.

Presence is fertile ground for organic fruit. Everything comes forth from Presence as perfectly ripe. The deeper, richer our immersion in Presence, the richer and more fruitful our words and actions emerging from it.

Virtue is an organic by-product of Presence. Excellence in any activity is both a result of and a reflection of our depth of Presence. The most superlative accomplishments resulting from the most strenuous effort will not have the same quality as actions flowing naturally, organically, effortlessly from a person practicing Presence.

Practicing Presence is akin to making maple syrup - the raw sap of the ego is boiled down again and again until only a heavenly sweetness remains.

Nothing issues from Presence without being as perfect as it can be. The more perfect our practice of Presence, the more unselfconsciously perfect our words and actions.

Presence is the space in which things become second nature for us. In Presence, we do things connaturally, i.e., without needing to think about them. Presence is where we let things happen instead of trying to make things happen. Presence is the space in which the music plays the master, not the master the music.

Presence is the space of discernment. In Presence, wisdom arises as thinking is set aside. Emotions do not disappear in Presence but are purified of their ego-dramatics. We see things more clearly, including the character defects of ourselves and others, but our reactivity to these is less. Critical judgment is anesthetized. Actions emerging from Presence exhibit a gentle, understanding decisiveness.

Presence is the space of personal 'ownership.' In Presence, we 'own' our problems, emotions, fears and mistakes, yet they lack the power to define or control us. In Presence, we make the shift from accusation to acceptance.

Every irritation is a summons to Presence. So too every form of unhappiness: resentment, anger, self-pity, grief, etc. Our awareness of these movements of dissatisfaction is a our call to rise above them. The moment we shift from being the victim to our emotions and become their observer, the manure life throws at us becomes fertilizer for our spiritual growth.

Presence is the spiritual alchemy that turns the heavy lead of life's problems into the pure gold of spiritual bliss.

Presence beautifies everything placed within it. Even evil, which is always a privation of something good, is viewed only with grief, not with anger, in the experience of Presence.

Presence saves us from identifying ourselves with the voices in our heads. Thinking is still operative in Presence - more perfectly operative than ever, in fact - but it determines nothing. Instead, an intuitive discernment arises when we are fully present, from which the right next word or action emerges naturally, spontaneously. Often the next right thing is to do or say nothing.

Even when we are stuck in ego, identified with the thoughts in our heads, often the best way forward is simply to keep our eyes and ears open and our mouths shut. When in doubt - which is always where we are when not practicing Presence - do nothing.

The only time trouble arises is when we lose our connection with Presence. In Presence, we have no troubles, only challenges that are opportunities for a deeper experience of Presence.

When we become aware of what our mind is saying - usually with its critical or accusatory judgments - we immediately behold the silliness of it all. We experience an instant, transcendent release, which is the advent of Presence.

Presence is our ever-available port in the storms of life. We can escape the tumult and fury of the changing winds in the world by averting to Presence. Presence beckons us like a lighthouse the endangered seamen; or, better yet, as a parent welcoming their child back from war.

Presence engenders in those who have discovered it an immense gratitude for finding this 'pearl of great price' (Mt. 13:46). It also gives them heartfelt compassion for those who, still banging their heads against the walls of the world, have not.

We need search no further for God than to become fully present to ourselves or others. Where even one person practices Presence, the glory of God shines forth and beautifies the world.

In Presence, synergy among persons is most electric. Ideas, associations, and creative connections occur more spontaneously, more powerfully in Presence than anywhere else.

Presence is a space of expectant listening. A person in Presence is the child listening for Santa Claus, the bride awaiting the bridegroom (cf. Mt. 25:2-13). Presence is the heart awake to the revelation of being.

Presence is an exercise in spiritual aikido. Every oppositional movement, internal or external, is welcomed, embraced, and leveraged in a synchronous whirlwind of beauty. In Presence, even our so-called sins, seemingly as black as carbon, are immortal diamonds just waiting to be unearthed.

Presence issues in the most delicate gentleness and the most unbreakable resolve. In Presence, self-confidence is both dissolved and strengthened. Presence deconstructs the ego in order to liberate the spirit. True personal identity is tacitly discovered through the purifying power of Presence.

Presence makes us wiser, not more clever. Presence inspires, whereas cleverness aims at impressing. The fragrance of inspiration, made possible in Presence, persists long after the mist of quick-wittedness has evaporated.

Presence anoints our words and actions with unction and gravitas, but in a way that is also light-hearted and easy to take. Those listening to or watching a person acting in Presence sense a seriousness that is as inviting as it is important.

Presence is the source of a spiritual intelligence, of which Artificial Intelligence (AI) is incapable. Presence is able to delight in the genius of AI, while also illuminating its inherent blindness. AI can never rejoice in its own genius, never experience a blissful awareness of itself as a gift of an Other. Presence, on the other hand, is nothing else than blissful awareness of the miracle of existence.

Presence mimics nothing, Artificial Intelligence mirrors everything. Artificial Intelligence is a house of mirrors, capable of imitating anything and everything. Presence, by contrast, is a pellucid window on eternity, in which nothing artificial appears.

In Presence, we can never be anything other than ourselves. Presence is not simply the death of the ego, it is an epiphany of awareness in which ego is inconceivable. Presence is a mystical space in which we discover our unfiltered selves.

Presence is not the opposite of anything. Presence is the unconditioned background of silence in which the world of opposites is immediately hushed.

Presence is the power of divinity burning like a perpetual vigil light in the deepest recesses of our being. It can never be extinguished, as it is the Light of God from which our very existence is derived.

Presence is the light which banishes the darkness of ego. Presence is the key that frees us from mental imprisonment. Presence is the volcano of hope, promise and bliss that blows apart anything that is placed over it.

Presence is pure attentiveness, unassuming and transparent as water, and just as life-giving.

Presence is only ever experienced as an epiphany, a revelation, a sudden arising of heightened awareness in which all things appear as being just as they are meant to be. Presence is an experience of Now - the eruption of eternity into time.

Presence moves mountains, i.e., mountains of fear, doubt, insecurity. Presence levels every mental hill and fills in every emotional valley. Presence turns the ups and downs of life into a delightful journey towards a horizon promising infinite joy.

Presence generates communion, just as granting freedom engenders intimacy. Presence is intentional letting-be-ness, and love arises in this space of letting be.

Presence communicates a 'there-for-you-ness' to the other. In Presence, persons feel loved, welcomed, accepted. Good behavior is a by-product of exposure to Presence.

Presence is mystical WD-40, loosening the most rusted-out bolts on our character armor. Presence fees us from the suffocating overlay of egoic identity.

Presence allows us to experience the world as if in slow motion, while also allowing us to accomplish more in less time. Presence enhances both our appreciation and efficiency.

Presence is an existential experience of death and resurrection. In Presence, we die to thoughts and expectations and are made alive to insights and epiphanies. Presence is a suspension of analysis and the advent of inspiration.

Presence makes all things new. In Presence, the flow of the world becomes not repetitive but kaleidoscopic - ever changing, ever new, ever more beautiful and intriguing. In Presence, nothing ever strikes us the same. In Presence, boredom is impossible. In Presence, we are continually arrested by the singularity of the Now.

Philip Krill

Presence fills us with an abiding sense of gratitude. In Presence, every form of light and darkness is apprehended as a gift. In Presence, lemons and lemonade are indistinguishable. In Presence, we see no evil, hear no evil, or speak no evil. In Presence, it's impossible to go wrong. In Presence, it's impossible not to be joyful.

Presence brings calm to the worst crisis, peace to the most disturbing situation. Presence is non-reactive, immediately giving pause to those caught in a world of reciprocal violence. Where tit is not returned for tat, tat doesn't know what to do with itself.

They who punch and lash out against persons practicing Presence do so in vain. They end up punching air and exhausting themselves in a futile effort to generate a reaction. They finish in an egoic collapse resembling that of a deflated blow-up toy.

Presence is a sacred place in which all things appear as inviolate. In Presence, it is impossible to harm anything or anyone. Presence is an inner sanctuary of pure veneration, of supernal reverence. In Presence, no one wants to have their cake and eat it too. In Presence, possessiveness is absent and appreciation abounds.

In Presence, we instinctively know when enough is enough. Presence produces an economy of words and actions, while expanding the space between them.

In Presence, limitations seem a fullness, finiteness infinitely perfect. In Presence, poverty is wealth, emptiness a *plērōma*.

Presence is an infinite horizon within which everything appears right sized.

Presence requires, produces and expands our patience. Presence demands we slow down, stop, look, and listen. Presence generates a desire to linger, to have a good, long look, to resist rushing off to the next pressing thing. In Presence, we realize the world will wait as we savor a taste of eternity.

In Presence, the right words come, the story writes itself, the perfect note is stuck, the song sings itself.

Presence is as commanding as it is self-effacing. Presence imbues our words and actions with arresting gravitas, while also filling us with childlike gratitude. Presence brings with it a sense that 'it has me,' I 'don't have it.'

Presence is a form of divine possession. Demonic possession is being possessed of the need to demonize. In the divine possession of Presence we are made incapable of accusation, indictment or scapegoating. Presence expels the demons of deception and division, of rivalry and resentment, of criticism and condemnation. In Presence, we even refuse to demonize the demonizers.

Presence arises like a Phoenix from the ashes in the crash-and-burn sites of our lives. The moment we recognize ourselves as acting crazy, we are no longer insane. The moment we acknowledge our failures, mistakes and weakness, the more powerfully Presence possesses, strengthens and transfigures us.

Presence the size of a mustard seed produces more abundant and exquisitely delicious fruit in our lives than the millions of artificially grown ideas and projects cultivated in the hothouse of our mind (cf. Mt. 13:31).

Presence is beyond 'is and is not.' Presence is unnameable yet undeniable. Every effort to question the existence of Presence assumes and affirms it. Yet, Presence can no more be captured than the air around us, or the shadow behind us.

Presence is a perpetual Big Bang of uncreated Light issuing forth from the indefinable center point of the present moment.

Presence cannot be hurt, but in Presence we can acknowledge and take ownership of our hurts. Ownership is symbiotic with being present. In Presence, responsibility and self-acceptance occur instantly, simultaneously and automatically.

We come into our own in Presence, while seeing clearly that our self-possession is a gift from a power greater than ourselves.

Thinking cannot lead us into Presence, but in Presence we are led into right thinking. Similarly, practicing virtue cannot make us present, but in Presence we become virtuous as a by-product of Presence.

Presence is the place where chaos exhausts itself. Presence is the space which quells turbulence and stills the storms of life. In Presence, the choppy waters of thoughts and emotions are smoothed out into a flowing stream of peace.

In Presence, we become the transcendental observer of our own thoughts and emotions. We stand outside them, as it were, experiencing ourselves as infinitely more than the waves in our brains or the voices in our heads.

Presence makes complaining impossible. Presence is the space of uncontaminated acceptance, not a space of intentional stupidity, as if the problems of our lives are not evident, but a space of infinite illumination in which the tumult of the world melts away like ice and snow in the noonday sun.

Presence prevents us from giving anything other than what is given to us in Presence. Presence reveals the emptiness of words and actions disconnected from itself. The power of Presence is what allows an author or a composer to tear up what they have written if they hear a single discordant passage in what they have produced.

Philip Krill

Everything that is good and produces good fruit comes as a by-product of Presence. It is never *what* is said that ultimately matters, only the Presence *with which* it is said. It is never *what* is achieved, only the manner *in which* it was achieved. Presence is the heart and soul of all that manifests as beautiful, true or good in this world.

Presence lifts us up, out and away from the quicksand of unconsciousness, establishing us firmly in our concrete, limited, ever-diminishing finitude to be glowing filaments of this power of Presence that transcends us.

Presence has nothing in common with ordinary thinking. The tangle of analysis is unknown in Presence. Presence is beyond balance, beyond paradox, beyond comparisons. Presence has no opposite. Presence is what it is - the source of our capacity to transcend ourselves from a place of bliss at the heart of who we are.

Presence generates a diminished need to explain or argue with anyone about anything. In Presence, we waste no time wrestling with the world. Instead, we desire only to help divinize the world by remaining in Presence.

The silence of Presence is a mystical fullness. The experience of Presence fills us with a bliss that is so simple, so virginal, so utterly disarming that we feel that no expression can do it justice.

Presence makes us exceedingly humble yet fills us with an unbounded confidence, not in ourselves but in the power of Presence that possesses us. In Presence, we experience a trustful surrender to an infinity of goodness beyond anything we can conceive of or express.

In the womb of Presence, we come to re-birth as new creations. In Presence, the cataracts that becloud our spiritual vision are removed and we can see again with the unsullied wonder and delight of a child.

The more we abide in Presence the more we have to say but less a desire to say it. Presence saturates us with such supernal bliss for which words seem either unnecessary or insufficient.

Presence makes communion possible. Presence is the mystical power that reveres otherness while preventing alienation. Presence is the supernatural energy that honors differences but allays divisions. Presence facilitates the happy marriage of freedom and love, unity and diversity. Presence brings peace where, otherwise, only antinomies exist.

Presence is an anticipation of an infinite fullness at a mystical end point of creation where Now and Forever are joined.

Presence is a fullness of Life which is never finished giving itself. The fullness of Presence consists in its self-dispossession. Presence, it seems, needs us to be filled with Presence as part of its own self-fulfillment.

Entering Presence from the gravitational pull of the ego is like a rocket ship breaking free from the earth's atmosphere. Once the invisible barrier of the egoic realm is broken through, we experience an incomprehensible peace, serenity, and breathtaking vision. The awe of the first astronauts is nothing compared to that of those who have broken through the atmosphere of egoic thinking into the space of perfect Presence.

Presence is the very definition of love: an invisible, unassuming, elusive, agenda-less openness to the other, devoid of expectations, filled with attentive awareness, inspiring connectivity, oozing with kindly regard, yet woven also with sagacity, keen discernment and an abundance of prudence.

In Presence, we simultaneously come home to ourselves and go beyond ourselves. In Presence, we are affirmed in our finitude through our openness to the Infinite. Presence elevates us and grounds us at the same time.

Presence is the silence in every silent night. Presence is the sacred, invisible halo enveloping and interpenetrating the cosmos. Presence makes everything alive in its own mode of consciousness. Presence is what allows even stones to speak.[17]

---

[17] See above, n. 1.

Presence always draws us back from the abstract into the existential. Presence always brings us back to the immediate moment, keeping us from walking too far down memory lane or wandering off into an unknown future. Presence always awakens us to the everything of the Now.

Presence uses creation as a sacramental catalyst to get us to attend, fully and completely, to what is right in front of our noses. By inviting us to contemplate the gratuity of what is given in the present moment, Presence awakens us to ourselves as those whose deepest bliss is simply to behold.

We will know that Presence possesses us when we awaken to the blissful realization that we have nowhere to go but here. We will experience the truth of the poet who said, *'the end of all our exploring will be to arrive where we started and know the place for the first time.'*[18]

What we do as persons in Presence flows from who we are as persons of Presence. Presence is the deepest essence of being human. We are singular mysteries of self-aware self-transcendence, in communion with each other, indissolubly bonded without confusion by the power of Presence. In Presence, 'we live and move and have our being' (Acts 17:28). Salvation' is our awakening to the blissful realization that we are 'gods in God' (Ps. 82:6; cf. Jn. 10:34-35).

Presence imparts infinite patience, while also sharpening our sense of timing. In Presence, we know when 'enough is enough,' yet we also learn how to set limits without doing damage to our relationships.

---

[18] T. S. Eliot, 'Little Gidding,' in his *Four Quartets*.

Regardless of what we perceive in Presence, we are filled with hope at the fecundity of the present moment. Every instant of unfiltered awareness casts a redemptive light on whatever is taking place within it.

Abiding in Presence we acquire certain gifts and virtues otherwise unachievable for us. Love, joy, peace, patience, kindness, goodness, faithfulness, gentleness, self-control - these are the fruits of being immersed in Presence. Nothing is ever 'achieved' in Presence, but many things we thought impossible for us are received.

There is a sense in Presence that we can always go deeper. Presence is, as it were, 'deep calling to deep' (Ps. 42:7).

The fontal mystery of Presence is not to be identified simply with our internal observer. Our first discovery of Presence is often that of being able to 'catch ourselves' doing or saying something we wish we hadn't. In so doing, we awaken to the realization that we have, as it were, a 'higher self,' an internal witness who remains blissfully unaffected by the egoic self. For many, this is a revolutionary realization, as indeed it is. But this is not the whole of Presence. Presence is infinitely more than awareness of ourselves. It is even more than our 'awareness of our awareness.' Presence is the transcendental mystery that makes this infinitely expanding 'awareness of our awareness' possible. Presence reveals our internal observer to be a finite instantiation of itself (Presence). We are finite creatures capable of infinite self-transcendence, made possible by a pre-existing source of Presence infinitely greater than ourselves.

Some practice Presence knowingly, intentionally and fairly continually, while others stumble into Presence now and again, feeling the immense relief that always comes with the momentary deliverance from egoic thinking, but they have no idea what happened or how to get back there. Everyone experiences the miracle of Presence whenever their thinking process either breaks down or temporarily ceases, but not everyone grasps what is happening or knows how to extend it.

Abiding in Presence, we extend Presence. Or, better, Presence radiates through us, beautifying that which is around us and awakening others to the movement of Presence within themselves.

As persons conscious of consciousness, we are unique instantiations of a Power greater than ourselves which is also the heart and soul of who and what we are. This Power is the ineffable mystery of Presence.

Presence works in and through us to transfigure the world with its own uncreated Light. It's almost as if Presence needs the world - and us - to manifest its pre-eternal power.

Immersed in Presence, we remain mute when others approach us with arguments, skepticism or sometimes even questions. The grammar of Presence has no points of contact with the mental and emotional syntax of the world. The internal operating system of those abiding in Presence is completely other from that of those immersed in thinking. The only question that ever arises in Presence is, 'Who's asking?'.

In Presence, we realize that our cognition is the receiver, not the generator, of our consciousness. In Presence, we sense that our brains are the antennae for, not the origin of, insight and inspiration. Presence intuitively reveals the illusion of materialism without wishing to argue the point.

We are not epiphenomena of Presence, yet Presence manifests itself in and through us in epiphanal ways. Presence alights within us, illuminating our entire being with peace, joy, and gratitude, whenever it pierces the darkness of our tunnel vision. Presence always possesses us as with a bit of surprise.

For those abiding in Presence, the notion and logic of 'explanation' seems to violate the mystery of being. To 'explain' something is to want 'to get a handle on it,' but reality refuses to be handled. Instead, the surfeit of being casts off all such 'explanations' and manifests itself as an infinite excess of Presence.

Abiding in Presence is its own reward. Presence reveals that nothing is simply a means to an end. The notion of 'ends and means' dissolves in Presence. All is seen to have a symphonic, kaleidoscopic integrity in which the whole and parts, the beginning and the end are mutually constitutive.

More deftly than a surgeon's scalpel, Presence cuts through the ephemeral to get to the heart of the matter. Imparting a vision not unlike that of a heart surgeon, Presence allows us to view even life-threatening situations with compassionate detachment. In Presence, we know almost instantly what to do, or not to do, to be most helpful in any situation.

Presence is a space of childlike joy. Every moment seems a new adventure, a further step in to a *plērōma* of promise. The more we practice Presence, the more blissful we become, and the more others experience our presence as a blessing.

Presence inclines us towards a less-is-more approach to life. Being present, we realize, is the 'pearl of great price' in life (cf. Mt. 13:46). The longer we abide in Presence, the more tawdry and unnecessary seem the pursuits and possessions that formerly gave us meaning.

In our experience of beautiful things, we sense that our beholding of them is even more beautiful than the things themselves. We come to realize it's not that beauty is in the eye of the beholder, but that the beholding itself is more beautiful than the beautiful things appearing within it.

Presence turns problems into immediate opportunities for deeper letting-go, for deeper letting-be. The more we practice Presence, the fewer our departures from it, and the more quickly such departures compel us to return.

Every time we return to Presence we do so with gratitude. Returning to Presence, even after a brief sojourn in the desert of unconsciousness, feels like drinking from a divine oasis.

Presence oozes from the virginal point in the abyss of our being, inexorably dissolving our layers of egoic overlay, eventually divinizing the whole of the human person. Once deified, persons saturated with Presence beautify the world simply by being themselves.

Presence turns us into watchdogs of the spirit. Presence sharpens our internal sense hearing so acutely that the slightest disturbance of spirit awakens us like mastiffs fully alert to an intruder. Presence guards the purity of heart of those possessed of it more jealously than a German shepherd its master.

Presence transforms us into virtuosos attuned to the soundings of the spirit. The tiniest discordant note of argument, irritation, resentment, etc., undetected by the egoic ear, seems sacrilegious. Immersed in Presence, we pray for the grace to do nothing to disturb its possession of us.

A person familiar with Presence can detect the power of Presence, as well as the lack of it, in the simple movements of another. Presence manifests itself in the way we walk, the way we talk, the way we look at others. Presence makes us unhurried and non-compulsive in our behaviors, even when we are inspired and excited. Presence makes us appear self-possessed and in complete control precisely because, in order to abide in Presence, we let go of control and surrender our egoic selves completely.

If Presence enables us to detect the lack of Presence in another, it does so after the manner of its own munificence. Presence transmutes our negative perceptions into prayers, our unflattering observations into oblations. Presence infuses us with an abiding sense of 'but for the grace of Presence, there go I.'

Living in Presence is akin to riding in a self-driving car. An intelligence far beyond our own negotiates the twists and turns of life for us while we relax in another world, aware of but undisturbed by the road rage we see all around.

Presence re-calibrates our emotional thermostat such that it kicks on immediately whenever our internal temperature rises or falls in the slightest degree. Presence alerts us instantly to the tiniest fluctuation in our affective function. Because it is self-regulating, Presence enables us to by-pass analytical analysis and return effortlessly to a resting place of dynamic equilibrium.

In Presence, we are rendered incapable of discussing or criticizing the faults of others. It's not that we don't notice them, but they are enveloped in such a penumbra of plenteous acceptance that we are ashamed even to think of them. Presence purifies everything it alights upon, most of all our hearts.

Presence requires we put on blinders to the eye candy of the world, as well as to the darkness of deception that overshadows the world. Presence focuses our attention within, drawing us into the deepest center of our being where we experience ourselves as a gift. Abiding in this virginal point of self-presence, gratitude is the only attitude we are capable of.

Presence is a silence pregnant with an infinitely personal, ultra-benevolent attentiveness. Others come to birth in the silence of our attentive acceptance.

Presence is a space of unconditional acceptance, a mystery of affirmation beyond approval or disapproval. When we are fully present, a validation of the other's intrinsic goodness arises. Presence awakens us to the primordial beauty of another's being. Presence is an epiphany of a transcendent love that makes moral judgments neither right nor wrong, but simply irrelevant.

Presence deconstructs the 'us vs. them' mentality. Presence creates a 'we' amidst the carnage of 'you' vs. 'me', 'mine' vs. 'yours. In Presence, differences are embraced while divisions are dissolved. In Presence, otherness is celebrated while oppositionalism is obliterated.

In Presence, even the innocent practice of giving our opinion seems presumptuous. Speculation seems sacrilegious, standing on principle, pontificating. Every form of interpretive commentary seems to do violence to the virginity of simply being.

Presence is filled with compassion towards those who are suffering because they are oblivious to the depths of their own self-transcendence.

Presence is the invisible arena of goodness in which evil exhausts itself. Presence is an ocean of mercy in which those who relax find themselves floating, and those who struggle find themselves drowning.

Presence is the wellspring of humility - so imperceptibly immanent that it fully transcends our ability to comprehend it, so unassumingly available that it seems non-existent.

Indiscernible by empirical observation, Presence is the very condition of our desire to understand. Presence eludes our every attempt to describe it, but inspires our hunger to do so. Presence is the source and satisfaction of our every yearning. Presence can never be grasped but has us continually in its grasp.

Presence affords us a keen appreciation of our limitations and finite capabilities, while imbuing us with a joyous acceptance of them. Presence inspires us to embrace our insufficiencies as an expression and recognition of its superior power within us.

Presence allows us to embrace ambiguity. Presence is the silent, unseen backdrop that renders every form of confusion undisturbing.

Insights appear in Presence like electronic waves and particles materialize in a quantum vacuum. They pop in and out of our awareness like the spiritual epiphanies they are.

When Jesus says, 'Stay awake!' (Mt. 24:42) he is referring to the vigilance required to benefit from the divinizing epiphanies that manifest themselves in Presence.

Presence is an infinite wellspring of blessing. Grace upon grace breaks in upon us when we abide in the alert, empty, attentive awareness of Presence. Contemplation is intentional openness to the wholly transcendent.

We might prefer the term 'Presence' to that of 'God' when pointing to the ineffable Source of our existence. 'Presence,' more so than the word 'God,' communicates the primordially personal mystery which names itself 'I AM' (Ex. 3:14). The Mystery of 'God' is ironically preserved when we forget about using the word 'God' when alluding to it.

The deeper we enter into Presence, the more peaceful we become. In Presence, inner stillness permeates our souls. Unceasing benevolence then arises from our unseen depths and inundates our demeanor and actions.

In Presence, failure does not exist. Presence imparts a sense of always beginning anew. Presence is the space in which hope springs eternal. Presence is the *Ur-grund* of redemption.

Presence is the invisible bond creating the so-called 'communion of saints.' Presence is the cheerful atmosphere in the local tavern where everybody knows your name. Presence makes for community amidst an atomized humanity.

Presence is the existential equivalent of the last judgment. In the bliss of Presence, we awaken to the fact that we've made our final judgments.

Presence is the unassuming revelation of death and resurrection as a single, existential mystery. When we die to our resentments, we rise in reconciliation. When we let go of our judgments, we receive unadulterated joy. When our holding on comes to an end, a rising above takes place.

In Presence, we experience the truth of St. Augustine's prayer: *Late have I loved You, O Beauty, so ancient, and yet so new! So late have I loved You! For behold, You were inside me, but I was outside, and sought you there. I, unlovely, rushed heedlessly among the things of beauty that You had made. You were with me, but I was not with You. Things kept me far from You, which would not have been, if they had not been in You. You called, and cried aloud, and broke open my deafness. You gleamed and shined, and chased away my blindness. You breathed out odors, and I drew in my breath, and now I breathe heavily for You. I tasted, and now I hunger and thirst. You touched me, and I burned for Your peace.*[19]

---

[19] *The Confessions*, Book 10, chapter 27.

Our joy is as complete as our rootedness in Presence. Anchored in Presence, we are at home. Established in Presence, we are immoveable in spirit. Abiding in Presence, there is nowhere else we would ever want to be.

Presence reveals our personal stories largely as chronicles of wasted time. Yet it does so with an impish smile. Knowing what we know in Presence makes everything else we thought we knew, or should have known, seem humorous.

Presence is a listening to, and a beholding of, the other that affirms the fundamental. goodness of the other in a way no words or actions can do. Being precedes doing - an ontological fact that is manifest most palpably in the experience of Presence.

The unction of altruism is anathema in Presence. Presence is what arrives after do-gooders have done their thing.

Great things seem possible in Presence, yet aspirations to greatness are a betrayal of Presence. Presence brings an infinite confidence resulting in infinite humility. In Presence, we sense that we can do all things, but through a power greater than ourselves.

Presence is the virginal womb in which our true selves are conceived, gestate and come to full term. Even as adults, we are renewed day by day within the womb of Presence.

Presence allows us to see the superfluous in our lives. Presence inclines us to an increasingly abstemious, less acquisitive lifestyle. Presence reveals possessions more as burdens than blessings. Presence prepares us to travel more lightly through life, forming us as pilgrims for eternity.

Presence frees us from our fears, even in times of tribulation. The peace of the present moment prevents the paralysis of fear. It's when we lose touch with the power of the Now that fear floods back in and overwhelms us. As complete, self-forgetful attentiveness, Presence is perfect love, and 'perfect love casts out all fear' (1 Jn. 4:18).

Presence is the indefinable point where a pirouette of peace takes place.

In Presence, the profit motive has no place, notions of success and failure have no meaning. Presence is a space of equanimous poise that mocks the pursuit of pleasure.

Presence is a transcendental membrane protecting our true selves from the vagaries of the ego. Presence is an invisible force field shielding our hearts from the deceptions of our minds.

Presence is a relinquishment of self-interest resulting in immediate deification. The shift from thinking to simply being present is an instant and indefinable transition from death to life, from ego to spirit, from darkness to light. It is as subtle and delicate as it is astounding.

Presence is an apophatic wellspring of inspiration and imagination. True creativity arises only within Presence.

Entering Presence is like entering the cathedral of the spirit. Humility and quietude, reverence and respect are its natural effects. Presence inspires an automatic purity of heart and stillness of mind that exclude the ego and cause our souls to soar.

Bottlenecks in our thinking prompt us to return to Presence. Backing away from the conundrums of our minds, we find immediate rest for our souls. Solutions to our problems present themselves most convincingly when, paradoxically, we have ceased searching for them.

Presence introduces a dimension of softness into the most serious situations. Presence never makes light of anything, yet makes all situations lighter.

In Presence, we taste eternity. In Presence, we are filled with fathomless joy, an abyss of appreciation. In Presence, the gratuity of being illumines everything we behold. In Presence, everything is holy.

Presence gives us the intuition that, in the end, 'all will be well, and all manner of things will be well.'[20] Presence discloses, in an anticipatory way, that we are all destined for joy.

Presence is at once the end of religion and the fulfillment of it. Presence actualizes within us the trust (faith), love and hope at which religion aims. In Presence, we acquire the 'purity of heart' that is 'the one thing needful' to experience God (cf. Mt. 5:8; Lk. 10:42).

In Presence, the kingdom of God opens within us. We see that it includes all others as well, whether they realize it or not.

Presence opens us to the griefs and joys of others, while preventing us from getting absorbed by them. Presence is the source of empathy and the antidote to codependence.

---

[20] See above, n. 3.

Connecting with Presence is the source of all holiness. Presence is an existential experience of salvation. In Presence, we are delivered from the antinomies and anxieties of the ego. In Presence, we are electrified, as it were, with a light and a love that makes our words and actions radiate with gentle power and humble conviction.

Presence reveals sin to be more silliness than serious. Sin is a loss of focus, a fall into egoic unconsciousness. In Presence, we view our sins as little more than wasted time.

Presence is the magnifying glass of God's Light. Presence focuses God's uncreated Light into a stream of living fire that burns away our ego and illumines our hearts with the infinity of God's love.

Presence is the golden thread of *kairos* connecting the otherwise meaningless events of *chronos*. Life is a cacophony of 'sound and fury signifying nothing' until we discover the redemptive power of Presence. Presence allows us to pierce the veil of chronological time and experience eternal life amidst our most mundane moments.

Abiding in Presence, we bring the sweet fragrance of God's love into any situation. Immersed in Presence, we are transfigured by God's uncreated Light. In Presence, we surprise ourselves with what comes out of us.

Presence makes us translucent and incandescent with a light and a love greater than ourselves. Presence is the space of our deification.

Presence is complete relinquishment resulting in complete fulfillment.

Abiding in Presence, we realize the truth of Jesus' words that 'the kingdom of God is within' (Lk. 17:21). 'When we've been there ten thousand years… we've no less days to sing God's praise than when we've first begun.'[21]

---

[21] See above, n. 7.